the issue is
LIFE

DEDICATED TO MY WIFE, BEVERLEY,
THE LOVE OF MY LIFE AND MOTHER
OF MY CHILDREN, WITHOUT WHOM
THIS BOOK WOULD NEVER HAVE
BEEN WRITTEN.

"For I know the plans I have for you," declares the Lord, "plans to prosper
you and not to harm you, plans to give you hope and a future."
Jeremiah 29: 11 (NIV)

Acknowledgments:

The writing of this book has not been a solo performance but a collaborative effort. Though I wrote it, I drew on the opinions and suggestions of many others.

The first thanks go to my family, especially my wife Beverley, who so encouraged me along the way from the very first time I suggested running for office. I could never have had the political career I had without her support and patience.

It was Dr. Bruce Wilkinson and his personal encouragement that gave me the idea to write this book. His mission to save babies is inspirational, and I thought this could be a handbook to help the cause.

I want to thank Pat Layton and Amy Madera who shared their personal stories and Rev. Fred Templeman, Cary Gaylord, Dr. Paul Enns, Beth Osborne and Whitney Waechter who, along with my wife, proofed and critiqued every word. Their suggestions were invaluable.

Rosemary Lester served as my editor and added so much to the flow of the book. Steven Lester of MindShift Publishing did the layout and publishing. I thank them both for their patience for my desire for perfection.

Lamar Vest has been a friend for years, and I am deeply indebted to him for writing the forward, as well as to the many others who added words of appreciation and endorsement.

Peter Rathbun, former President of The Christian Legal Society, was so helpful in reviewing the text from a legal standpoint.

My Pastor, Ken Whitten, has been one of my most ardent supporters and has cheered me on in this venture. I shall always be indebted to him for his encouragement and his shepherding my Christian growth.

Most importantly, I give thanks to God, who gave me this book. All I did was to transcribe it.

To God be the glory for the great things He has done.

WHAT OTHERS ARE SAYING

"John Grant understands that America will never be all it can be until we end the destruction of innocent, unborn children."

Gary L. Bauer,
Founder of Campaign for Working Families and former presidential candidate, Domestic Policy Advisor in the Reagan Administration

"The right to life is the right of all rights. It is the most important right that government and society should protect. Sadly, America adopted a culture of death in 1973 when the Supreme Court decided Roe v. Wade. John Grant clearly states the self-evident truth that Life is the Issue. I believe that this bloody chapter in American history will soon end and that we in America will adopt a culture of life to protect the most vulnerable among us from the moment of conception to natural death. May God forgive America and heal our land. May that blessed day come quickly. The Issue is Life is a must read. Through this book John Grant speaks for those whose voices have been muted and whose cries for mercy have been ignored. Each one of us should accept the challenge and boldly defend the defenseless."

Mathew Staver
Founder and Chairman, Liberty Counsel; Dean and Professor of Law, Liberty University School of Law

"John Grant has a passion for protecting the unborn, which he took into the public arena and now has put in his book. It is both an encouragement and a handbook to read for all who stand for the sanctity of life and desire to act to end abortion."

Eugene Habecker,
President, Taylor University

"Few have had a closer view than I of former Florida State Senator John Grant's pro-life work. While working with John as the Legislative Consultant to the Florida Baptist Convention for almost two decades, I personally witnessed much of what will be shared in this book; both professionally and personally. Senator Grant's legislative and family experiences plus his wise counsel concerning future advocacy for the Right-to-Life make this a must read for anyone dedicated to the Sanctity of Human Life."

William H. Bunkley
President, Florida Ethics & Religious Liberty
Commission, Inc.

"In an age where we place more value on oak trees, being prohibited from cutting them down, than we do on children, where mothers are allowed to kill their preborn children, Senator John Grant has written a timely, provocative book. He correctly understands the issue: there is life, a human being, at the moment of conception (Ps. 139:15-16). This is a biblical and moral issue. Abortionists claim it is a matter of choice. Whose choice? The baby has no choice in the matter. Some 55 million babies have died since Roe vs. Wade's horrible, immoral tragedy. Senator Grant speaks to the issue and his words should move the conscience of our nation's people that Roe vs. Wade would be reversed and life for the unborn be protected."

Paul Enns, Th.D.,
Author of *Heaven Revealed* and *Approaching God*
Professor, Southeastern Theological Seminary

"John Grant has written a powerful, personal, and needed defense of human life. Senator Grant speaks the truth with courage and passion and shows us how we can win this war for the unborn."

David Clarke, Ph.D.
Psychologist, speaker, and author of *Married But Lonely*

"To read this book is to know the heart of a man who has had years of personal experience in the trenches and front lines of the fight for the lives of the unborn baby who deserves to breathe air, pet puppies, see butterflies, blow out candles on birthday cakes, to love and to receive love."
　　Stephen Wise,
　　Florida Senator (Retired)

"I have known Senator John Grant for thirty-five years and during that time I have never seen him waiver on his passion for the Holy Bible, the sanctity of life, American politics and his family. I encourage anyone who has those same passions to read **The Issue is Life** *to see how one person can make a difference in the very difficult political arena in which we find ourselves today."*
　　Pieter Dearolf,
　　Chairman, American Bible Society

"John Grant has long been a force to stop abortion and this book is an important, timely and interesting source on the issue of abortion. It clears up many crucial issues in a clear and concise manner and should be read by all who are interested in an honest dealing with this topic!"
　　Rev. Fred Templeman,
　　Founder, Foundation Outreach Ministries

"The issue of abortion is 'ground zero' in the culture war, and Senator John Grant is no stranger to the fight. He has long been a powerful policy influencer in the political and legal arenas. This book gives voice to that journey and hope for victory ahead."
　　Rev. Steven Lester,
　　Pro-Life Keynote Speaker, CEO of Steven Lester Creative and MindShift Publishing

"For most of his life, John Grant has been a warrior against the culture of death. In **The Issue is Life***, he lays out the reality facing the Pro-Life movement in a skillful and practical way. More importantly, he shares wisdom gained from his life's experience and inspiration for those who would follow his lead."*
  Lisa Huetteman
  Author of the book: *The Value of Core Values*

John Grant is a real champion of Life. He shows how good legislation can be developed and passed into the kinds of laws that will honor God and serve our highest needs as a people."
  Susan Baldwin,
  Executive Director, The Women's Resource Center of Mobile

"John Grant has been a friend and ministry partner for the Sanctity of all Human Life for over 25 years. John is the real deal, a promise that is sometimes missing in our elected officials. His story will inspire you and stir you to either "stay the course" for life until it is finished or instill a passion to be a bigger part of this heart of God cause. John and his wife Beverley are dear to my heart, and I am honored to endorse this book and watch with them, how God will use it for His glory!"
  Patricia Layton,
  Founder and President, Life Impact Network,
  Author of *Surrendering the Secret* and *A Surrendered Life*

"I have respected Senator Grant for many years for the courageous stand he has taken on the abortion issue, our national shame. He has done so in the face of strong opposition and without fear for the possible negative consequences to himself. His book **The Issue Is Life** *is an eloquent summary of his life's battle against the pro-choice forces in Florida and in America. In it he stands as a staunch defender of the rights of the unborn child, making a host of moral, Biblical, legal and social arguments to undergird his case, always returning to the fundamental issue that these innocent,*

defenseless little ones are living human beings. I recommend his work as a key resource for every legislator and judge who must make judgments about this critical issue and for every citizen who would make an informed judgment about his/her personal conviction in this matter."

Dr. H.E. "Buddy" Payne, Jr.
President, Florida College

"I know the plans I have for you declares the Lord." Yet for many, the question remains, "Am I willing to step into the plans God has for my life?" In the case of John Grant, the answer is a resounding YES! He and his wife Beverley have been called to serve God in many capacities, but none is more personal or passionate than being a voice for the littlest among us - the unborn! In this courageous book, John shows us how to step out and boldly add our voices to the issue of life! And through his tireless efforts, John is bringing wisdom to a world that desperately needs to know the truth."

Tom and Pam Wolf,
Co-founders of Identity and Destiny

"One of the saddest, darkest days in America's history was when nine Supreme Court Justices, appropriately dressed in black, decreed it was now legal for a woman to have her unborn baby put to death. But is the issue one of life or death? As you read this book, you hear a voice, a voice of compassion, a voice of conviction, a voice that comes to us from the womb and speaks for those whom we will never hear. It is the voice of experience and the voice of expertise. Senator John Grant speaks not only from law, but from love, and believes that while the debate seems to be one of death, the real issue is Life."

Ken Whitten,
Senior Pastor, Idlewild Baptist Church

"Come along with John Grant on his "journey of passion," a journey filled with grace and truth. While few of us may be called to battle in the legal arena in defense of the right to life, there is much that each of us can do to influence the hearts and minds of

our families, friends and colleagues. This book will encourage and equip you to do just that."
  Peter Rathbun,
  Past President, Christian Legal Society
  General Counsel, American Bible Society

"Growing up watching my father advocate for the life of the unborn, even when unpopular, helped prepare me to serve in the Florida House of Representatives. He showed me by example how to approach the legislative process with intellectual honesty, integrity, and humility."
  James Grant,
  Florida State Representative

"Senator Grant's book is a deeply passionate and thoughtful expression of his many years of commitment to the anti-abortion cause. For all those who have an investment in this issue – undeniably one of the most divisive social and political issues of our day – John's sincerity, candor, and insights will add new dimension to their perspective. I commend him for giving himself so fully to living by the convictions that are brought to him through his faith in Christ."
  The Reverend Luis Cortés Jr.
  President, Esperanza

This Issue is Life *is a must-read book for every American. Senator Grant convincingly makes the case that if you do not protect innocent life, all of our freedoms as Americans are jeopardized. Encourage your friends and neighbors to read this book and live out its message. Our founders fought for "life, liberty, and the pursuit of happiness." Let's take this book's challenge to this generation before it's too late.*
  Attorney David Gibbs III
  President, National Center for Life and Liberty
  Author, *Fighting for Dear Life: The Untold Story of Terri Schiavo and What It Means for All of Us*

The Issue Is Life, *encapsulates the issue of abortion in a soul searching manner to unmask, expose, and enlighten our weakest links in defending the sanctity of life. Senator Grant has been a long time, courageous champion for family, life and morality in the "real" battlefields, not in words alone.*

Linda Rossetti Brocato, MSE,
Author, founder of Brocato Publishing,
and co-founder of Prepare His Ways Ministries, Inc.

"John Grant is a man of influence, integrity and impact -- and yet he is first a family man and a man of God. His new book is a must read for all who believe in and want to protect the precious sanctity of human life."

Christopher Gould,
Vice President, Salem Communications Corp.

JOHN GRANT

Published by Steven Lester, dba MindShift Publications
Atlanta, GA
ISBN: 978-0-615-87441-8

Contents

FOREWORD

John Grant has gallantly fought for human rights throughout his illustrative personal, legal and political life. It is appropriate that he now stands up for the rights of the most vulnerable and helpless of our society: the unborn children.

I have known John Grant for more than twenty years. He has helped greatly to transform my opinion of politicians. From casual observations, politicians always seem to carefully pick their fights with an eye toward how the majority of the electorate might feel. Not John. He has always been guided by spiritual discernment which, by its simplest definition, is the ability to decide between truth and error, right and wrong. It is the ability to think biblically about all areas of life.

So, once again in writing this book John Grant has thrown himself into the heat of a battle that will not necessarily win friends and influence people in high places. That speaks loudly and clearly about his personal integrity, a hallmark of his life and career. As he has proven over and over again, personal integrity is a position, win or lose, he will not forfeit.

John and Beverley dealt with the issue of life and death up close and personally at the birth of their firstborn. They made the right decision. The facts and evidence that John shares in "The Issue is Life" will hopefully cause others to make the right decision. And, with hopeful anticipation, I pray that it will cause those who help make the laws of our land to see that the issue is really about life and early death, not about a simple choice.

As John Grant reminds us repeatedly in this book, "the abortion issue rises or falls on the matter of when life actually begins." The myth is that we really can't make that determination. As John indicates, both biblical and scientific evidence demystify that argument. The real issue centers on the debate as to whether this biological human being in the womb is a "person" worthy of rights and protection.

"*The Issue is Life*" does so much more than point out the dreadful results and effects of abortion. John gives practical steps for alternatives, especially in pointing out the incredible success of Crisis Pregnancy Centers across the USA, that, as Senator Grant shares, "not only help a mother to give birth, but they will also find her assistance if she wants to keep her baby, or help the mother find a good home for her child through adoption."

It seems obvious that no lasting change will ever take hold in our nation until those who truly believe that life is sacred and must be protected take a definite stand. John Grant makes that challenge to us in this book. He informs us that education is the first step in this long journey. May God use "The Issue is Life" to help us take giant steps in that journey.

R. Lamar Vest
Pastor, Times Square Church, New York City
Former President and CEO, American Bible Society
Former Chairman of National Association of Evangelicals
Former General Overseer of the Church of God
Former President of Lee University

INTRODUCTION

"And ye shall know the truth, and the truth shall make you free. "
-John 8:3

I have discussed it, debated it and fought for it, though I have never taken the time to put my thoughts in writing. This book is my attempt to do exactly that.

This book is written in order that the experiences of my life can help you in your life. The issue in the abortion debate is one that has divided our country more than any issue since slavery. It is an issue about life and about social and sexual freedom.

It is for me a matter of passion to save the lives of the hopeless and helpless for whom no one speaks. The unborn are the most helpless in our society, and their brutal demise is the ultimate of child abuse.

I ran for elective office and served for twenty-one years to make a difference, and for all that time my passion was to protect the lives of the unborn. While I feel that ultimate victory will have to be in God-changed hearts and minds of people, the battleground still remains before the courts and in legislative chambers across the land.

As part of a legislative body, I learned how to and how not to fight the battle, and I trust that this book will benefit others from the lessons I have learned.

The death count of aborted infants in the United States alone is well over fifty-five million since 1973, when abortion became legal. That is more than the population of the three largest states combined-New York, California and Texas!

The cost has been more than the loss of life. It has been socially divisive, morally destructive and economically disastrous. While Roe v. Wade dealt with abortion, its roots are much deeper. It forever changed our society. The issue is life and what we believe about it in all facets.

The decision created some rights for those outside the womb, but took away rights for millions still in the womb. It created a new industry and a changed mind-set. It said to people that if the court found it to be right, then it must be right. But what it created was a culture war between good and evil.

People, both those elected to office and citizens on the outside, ask me how they can make a difference. My intent in writing this book is to give them some answers.

I also have my own story to tell of why and how my wife and I came to the point of being so passionate about saving the lives of the unborn. Our story is sincere, true and resonates with even those who disagree with our position.

The news is not all bad. We are winning the battle, bit by bit, piece by piece and day by day. Public opinion is changing, though the media would deny it, as more people are informed as to the law, the issues, the process and the crisis. No war was ever won with a single battle.

The key is to remember that the issue is life. It is not a debate about sociology, economics or personal freedom, nor is it about when the conception occurs. The issue is the sanctity of God-given, God-breathed creation of human life, nothing more, nothing less and nothing else.

Abortion is nothing less than fetal homicide and is the ultimate form of child abuse.

Many people are becoming involved in the efforts to preserve the lives of the unborn and many more want to know how they can become involved to make a difference. There are now well over three thousand crisis pregnancy centers where women are ministered to and can learn both the cost and alternatives to abortion. Untold numbers, that only God knows, are being saved from the horrors of abortion.

These crisis pregnancy centers are our first line of defense. They run primarily on volunteer help, and their volunteers see the crisis firsthand and are challenged and motivated to become involved.

My reasons for writing this book are to empower people with the truth about abortion and to give a better understanding of how to dialogue with people of a different persuasion, especially those in political office.

I also hope this story will be an inspiration for those who might answer God's call to step up to the plate and take a swing at elective office. We can never expect the right answers when we elect the wrong people. The best way to secure the right votes on issues is to elect the right people before they take office.

Where truth is known, the persuasion for protection and rights of the unborn becomes clear and unambiguous.

John Grant
July 2013

CHAPTER ONE

A JOURNEY OF PASSION

"The only thing evil men need to triumph is for good men to do nothing"
-Edmund Burke

It began as a typical high school romance when two young kids met in the high school band. I was a senior and she a sophomore. Neither of us ever dated anyone else after that. We dated through the rest of high school, college, graduate school and partly through law school before we were married.

She had just graduated and earned her diploma in Elementary Education, and I was entering my second year of law school. She was my "blonde" scholarship. We were very much in love, and once my graduation and a job were in sight, we decided to start our family.

It didn't take long to find out that "we" were pregnant, and what a joyous occasion that was. Then the unthinkable happened. There was an outbreak of German Measles in her first grade class. It was a disease she never had as a child and, therefore, we became alarmed since we were expecting our first child. We knew a couple who had a baby after the mother had measles, and the child was born partially blind, deaf and deformed.

A visit to the doctor didn't calm our fears but did give us a choice. He said that my wife had been exposed at the most vulnerable time of her gestation. If she contracted measles, the baby definitely would, but even if she didn't, it was possible that the baby might.

He suggested an easy alternative ---- ABORTION----- but we didn't know what to think. This was before all the public debate and before abortion was legal. I knew what the term meant, but that was about all. I think the only time I heard the term in law school was a passing comment that it was illegal.

There were ways the doctor advised to get an abortion done, but we would have to cross international borders to have the procedure. He gave us all the social and economic reasons why we should have an abortion. He sent us home to think about it.

We arrived home frightened and confused. What he had said to us made so much sense, but we both had a check in our spirit. Though churched, neither of us had deep spiritual salvation roots. I would like to say that we prayed about it, but I have no recollection that we did.

A few nights later, as we sat on our sofa, I placed my hand on her abdomen and said "I wonder if it is a boy or a girl?" She responded, "I wonder if it is a healthy baby?" Together, we came to the conclusion that regardless, it was our baby. Whether it was a boy or girl, whether it was healthy or not, it was not our right to terminate the pregnancy of our baby. We both knew we had made the right decision.

The birth was easy and the baby was healthy. Today he is a handsome and talented lawyer with a beautiful wife and four children, the oldest of which is pictured on the cover of this book. I can't begin to count the times over the years that I have looked at him and thought about how close we had come to ending his life.

This experience left Beverley and me with a new-found sense of life in all its facets. Little did we ever dream that within five years the action of the United States Supreme Court would strike down most laws in the United States that prohibit abortions.

When the court acted, I, along with many others, was stunned. Something had to be done. It didn't take long for the new abortion industry to spring up across the land. It was well-funded and quickly became quite profitable.

There was also a tremendous academic and media driven campaign to change public opinion, and it was extremely successful. People were told that the "product of conception" was not a human life. They were told that it should be a woman's choice. They were told that abortion could save unwanted babies from being abused and reduce an economic drag on families and our society.

PEOPLE WERE TOLD THAT THE "PRODUCT OF CONCEPTION" WAS NOT A HUMAN LIFE. THEY WERE TOLD THAT IT SHOULD BE A WOMAN'S CHOICE. THEY WERE TOLD THAT ABORTION COULD SAVE UNWANTED BABIES FROM BEING ABUSED AND REDUCE AN ECONOMIC DRAG ON FAMILIES AND OUR SOCIETY.

Lower courts at the state and federal level, exercising a level of judicial activism never before experienced, handed down many decisions guaranteeing the right to privacy, even to minors who did not enjoy such privacy for other medical procedures.

State legislatures followed suit by enacting all kinds of "protective" legislation such as exempting abortion clinics from certain licensing, inspection and statistical reporting to which other facilities providing other medical procedures were subject.

Unfortunately, even though there was a nearly two year lapse between the first argument in Roe until the decision was handed down, those who would oppose open abortion got caught off guard. After all, even the first thirteen colonies and every state after that had laws opposing abortion. They never thought that a court would "legislate" from the bench, and they believed that any attempt to change the law would come from the legislative bodies.

In the late seventies, the "right to life" movement began, with many organizations under various names springing up throughout the nation. The term 'right to life' refers to the belief that a human being has an essential right to live and that an unborn child is a human being.

Right away the movement became somewhat muddled. Some extended it to include the right to life for the elderly and terminally ill, while some injected the issue of capital punishment saying that if one does not support abortion, one cannot support capital punishment.

At first that might seem to be a plausible argument and it was one I had to work through early in my career as a lawyer. I was a capital crimes prosecutor, which meant that I generally only prosecuted cases that carried the death penalty.

I have always believed, and still do, that the death penalty is a just penalty and a deterrent to crime. During my first capital trial, when the defense rested, the judge sent us all home to return the following morning to argue to the jury.

That night, as I prepared my argument, I suddenly broke out in a cold sweat realizing that I was going to stand before a jury the following morning and ask them to take a person's life. It was something I had never done.

I thought of how outspoken I had been about taking the life of the unborn and now would have to ask a jury to take a life. Was there a conflict? Of course not, I concluded.

The baby is innocent. The defendant was guilty of taking someone else's life. So much for that argument of the pro-choice group. Like most of their arguments, this holds little logic.

Meanwhile, my passion for protecting the unborn grew. How could I make a difference?

I now had a passion. The question was what I could do to satisfy my passion through my actions. The more important question was what I could do to repair a broken world.

One day, as I was venting my frustrations about some of these issues to a friend, he suggested that I run for a seat in the state legislature. I told him he was crazy, to which he responded that if I was not willing to run, I should stop complaining about the actions of those who do.

I like to tell people that I ran to get the right to complain. I won and spent the next twenty-one years complaining!

CHAPTER TWO

INTO THE FIRE

"Even so the tongue is a little member, and boasts great things. Behold, how great a matter a little fire kindles!"

-James 3:5

Once having decided to run for office, I took on a well-entrenched member, whose voting record was less than stellar. However, his political party made up seventy-two percent of the registered voters. The party of my registration was the party of less than a quarter of the members of the House of Representatives. The campaign would indeed be an uphill challenge.

Many who wanted to support me urged me to switch parties, saying that I couldn't win as a minority member and even if I did win, I would never be in leadership where I could make a difference. However, by this time, the majority party had accepted the pro-abortion position and swallowed it hook, line and sinker.

I told people that I would lose the election before I would win it with compromise.

It was late in the year, and I had no political organization or backing. In spite of my having a degree in political science and one in government, I knew absolutely nothing about running a campaign.

When in a tough battle, always commit it to the Lord. I went to the state capitol and walked into the House chamber, sat at my opponent's desk and prayed. I gave it all to God and prayed that win or lose, to Him be the glory.

Having been heavily involved in my denomination's men's ministry, I turned there to recruit help. Even though many of these men had never been politically involved, they stepped forward, and many of them are still involved thirty years later.

I told people I would not lose, because elected or not, I would speak out on the issues even if my position was unpopular. State-wide casino gambling was on the ballot that year and I spoke out against it, and we defeated it. But when I spoke out against abortion and told it like it was, I walked into a buzz saw by explaining abortion in a way many had not heard. I was able to bring many converts to our side. That was a victory in and of itself.

But at the end of the day, we failed to get elected by less than half of a percent of the votes cast. Several people called to remind me that I had said I would not lose. I told them that I did not lose. I just failed to get elected. I told them I had helped to defeat casino gambling, educated and recruited many for the pro-life cause and built a solid political organization for the future. I was astounded by all that had been accomplished in a short, six-month campaign in a district where demographically I should have been defeated by a two to one margin.

Not knowing what the future held, I returned to the practice of law and became more deeply involved in my church. I was uncertain whether or not my political career was over, but at least I had tried and had given it my all.

About a year and a half later, out of the clear blue and due to a resignation in the legislature, a seat opened up to be filled in a special election. The open seat was the one I had run for in the previous election. Immediately my phone began to ring off the hook. It was the same district, the same issues and the same disproportionate party registration. Moreover, being the only race on the ballot, the political parties would focus on it intensely, not wanting to lose a seat in a pivotal presidential election year.

Could I do it? Should I do it? Was it possible? Would I be willing to risk a second loss? Was now the right time? All of these questions raced through my head, as more people called to urge me on. By this time, the abortion issue had really escalated and was becoming a major issue in the presidential race. Governor Ronald Reagan was attempting to unseat President Jimmy Carter.

Reagan's party had not adopted a pro-life platform (that would take a few more years), but they hadn't rejected it either. But the President's party was clearly pro-choice, and people were beginning to notice that there was a difference.

I toyed with the idea of making the run. The worst that could happen would be that I would fail to get elected, but I knew I would have a platform from which to speak about the sanctity of human life. To help me with the decision, I hired a pollster and took a scientific poll.

The pollster came back to me with good news. I could win the race if I ran. However, he said I would need to make one minor adjustment. I would have to go pro-choice or at least neutral to win. There was no way I could win with a pro-life position in that year in that district. He said the real pro-life support was in surrounding districts, but not in the one where I lived.

Shocked, I looked at him and said, "You don't know me very well. I will run as a strong pro-life candidate and lose before I will compromise on my number one issue and passion to win."

" I WILL RUN AS A STRONG PRO-LIFE CANDIDATE AND LOSE BEFORE I WILL COMPROMISE ON MY NUMBER ONE ISSUE AND PASSION TO WIN."

After that conversation, I was fired up more than ever. I prayed about it and asked God first for wisdom. But then I asked Him to make the race so difficult that obviously only divine guidance could bring about a victory at the polls. How little did I know that He would honor that request so thoroughly.

I threw my hat in the ring, rounded up the army of volunteers from the first campaign, and we were off and running. In those days, e-mail and cell phones didn't exist, but I had a land line and three of the biggest Rolodex models I've ever seen all filled with names and contact information.

It was a hard-fought, neck-and-neck race, and we were out maneuvered on the surface. Since there was not another office holder in either of the two counties in my district, all the local officials endorsed and worked for my opponent. The Governor came into Tampa and in one fund-raiser raised more for my opponent than my total campaign budget in the first election.

I was able to spend time with Governor Reagan when he came to town. I introduced him on the platform, and he said some nice things about me from the palm card I had slipped in his coat pocket while we sat together on stage. That was great, but it didn't seem to make much of a difference since voters in his party were with me anyway....... all twenty-eight percent of my district's voters. What I needed was voters of the majority party.

The race seemed to be slipping away as we neared the finish line. But where God closes a door, He opens a window, and that window of opportunity happened in a rural east county town where my opponent and I were debating each other before the local Kiwanis Club.

When I realized that the debate was being covered by the Tampa Tribune, I knew that there would be a story to be read in the next day's edition, and it was time to make a move.

I had been carrying a document around in my pocket for some time and waiting for the right time to make it public. This was a document signed by my opponent regarding unionization of agricultural workers which stated a position I knew would not go over well in this small farming community.

I made sure the debate covered the issue and, as expected, my opponent's answer played to the home town crowd. On rebuttal, I pulled the document from my coat pocket and simply asked him which was his real position and when had he changed his mind from what he had previously stated when he signed this document.

It was the front page story in the next day's paper and was

read throughout the district. What really hit the voters was not particularly where he stood on the issue, but the fact that his lack of integrity had been exposed.

I have always advised candidates that personal integrity is what really matters most with most voters, as I will explain in greater detail in another chapter.

The tide began to change. Public officials began to call me and say I couldn't tell anyone they had called. They said they couldn't come out for me in support, but that certain people would be calling me with offers of help. And they did.

I never let up on the abortion stance. I told the voters it was not a stance from a political perspective because if it was, all the political indicators would encourage me to be pro-abortion.

With warmth and sincerity I told them about the son we almost aborted and how we came to believe what we believed. We told them that it was from my heart, not my head. Many who still disagreed with me gave me their support based on my sincerity and the fact that I didn't make decisions solely on which way the political wind was blowing.

The momentum was shifting, but none of the political pundits could explain why. After all, anyone who was anybody politically was on the other side. What they failed to see was the underground "God Squad" of churches and people who were working like bees in a hive.

It was still tight going into the election, but even God seemed to put his signature on the day of election. It was bright and sunny in the biggest minority party precincts, and yet it was raining cats and dogs everywhere else.

At the end of the day, I received two out of every three votes cast, and at midnight, I became the first of my party to be elected from my county to the Florida House of Representatives since the Reconstruction Era.

CHAPTER THREE

ON TO THE CAPITOL

For we are his workmanship, created in Christ Jesus unto good works, which God hath before ordained that we should walk in them.   *-Ephesians 2:10*

Coming off the high of winning the election was followed with the reality of rearranging my schedule, hiring a staff and finding a place to live near the state capitol.

At such a late date, housing was virtually non-existent. So I decided to go to a near-by campground and live in the family motor home. I drove up with the family and was accompanied by a Tampa Tribune reporter who wanted to use the four hour journey to interview me.

That same night, Beverley and I drove over to the capitol and went to the chamber of the House of Representatives. When we walked in, promptly a man introduced himself as the Sergeant-at Arms told me the chamber was closed and we would have to leave.

I told him that I had just been elected and was interested in where I would be seated. With apologies, he escorted me to my seat. The following morning, I rose from that seat and walked forward, held my hand on the Holy Bible and was officially sworn in as the newest and most junior member of the House.

Out of one hundred and twenty members in the House of Representatives, I became legislator number 32 on my party roster. I knew there was a lot of work to be done in order to become the majority party.

My election generated a lot of press. The editorial page described my election as a "harbinger of elections to come." I received a full front page picture in the Friday Extra section of the Tribune and a sizeable story inside. Being the first of my party to be elected to the House in over a hundred years was newsworthy. But the real story, as the abortion wars were heating up, was that a pro-life legislator could be elected from a district that polled two to one pro-choice, where three of every four voters were registered in a party with a pro-choice platform.

Indeed, it was a harbinger of things to come, and that scared the daylights out of many of the majority party leadership. Many of these leaders were embarrassed because they had told the lobby corps (often referred to as the third house) before the election not to worry because there was no way I could win.

I was assigned to a small office in the basement and named to minor committee assignments, but I had a vote button and microphone on the floor just like everyone else.

The majority party immediately began talking about recruiting a candidate against me in the next election, either a rematch with the man I defeated or another candidate. At the end of the day, the only candidate they could come up with was a bail bondsman. This man told me not to worry; he was running because the publicity he would receive was well worth the filing fee and cheaper than any paid advertising. In the next election, the majority party leadership recruited a man who ran a gas station. I won both elections by wide margins.

My pro-life passion had preceded me to the capitol and made many people uncomfortable. Even those who had run on a pro-life platform from more conservative districts would rather not bring the abortion issue up or have to vote on any "divisive" legislation. It was especially disconcerting to me to realize there were those who reasoned that in light of Roe v. Wade, they would not have to deal with abortion in a vote. They would freely tell people what they wanted to hear depending on the tilt of the audience.

Little did they all know that someone had come to town to talk about the horrors of abortion and how Roe not withstanding, something could be done about abortion piece by piece and inch by inch. Not everyone was happy about that, especially some self-proclaimed pro-lifers in my own party, who would just as soon use the issue to get elected but not have to touch it after that. They knew the issue is life.

People asked me how long I planned to remain in the legislature. I told them until the minority party becomes the majority party of the Governor and both houses of the legislature. Little did I know that it would take twenty-one years.

Over those years, I managed to win eight elections to either the House or Senate. Every election was a dog fight, because I had one of the most party vulnerable seats and always had a target on my back. Every election, the polls showed that on a generic poll, the district was significantly pro-choice.

In order to survive, I needed an incumbency protection program, especially to protect me from those who opposed my stand on moral and family issues. Some of what I did was just common sense and common courtesy.

Since I knew each race would be tough, I was in campaign mode year round. It was good, because it allowed me to stay in touch with the people of my district and gave me the opportunity to help them understand where I stood on issues and why.

I spoke at high school graduations and local civic and service clubs, swore in officers of the local ladies garden circle and went most anywhere I was asked to go.

When I was elected, one legislator gave me some good advice. He told me that if I answered my phone calls and responded to my mail, I would be okay. He also reminded me that I was a state legislator not a county commissioner and that I should stay out of local issues where at all possible. I followed his advice and it paid off.

I was courteous and non-confrontational with people who disagreed with me, even those who came to vehemently disagree with me. I always thanked them for being involved in the process. I also made sure that anyone who wanted an appointment with me received one.

This policy left the pro-choicers scratching their heads. I always greeted them with open arms, which was something many other pro-life legislators refused to do. I politely listened to their positions and explained mine. I made sure they knew I understood that politically it would be better to be on their side to run for election in my district, and I would take the time to tell them the story of how my wife and I almost aborted our son and how that decision brought me to my position. As I scanned their faces, I could see those with tears in their eyes and I knew those who had experienced an abortion.

There are many women's issues other than abortion, and I tried to be as supportive of those issues as I could. I introduced and passed the Anti-Stalking Act, funding for osteoporosis, and mandatory insurance coverage for diagnostic mammograms, as well as the Corrections Equality Act and others.

When the National Organization of Women, Planned Parenthood and other similar groups would present their candidate screening, I would always attend. This was something many pro-life legislators and candidates would not waste their time doing. Each time, the interviewers would shake their head and question why I attended their meetings. I wanted them to know I was with them on practically every issue on their agenda except for the one that was the litmus test.

They knew my position without asking, and I knew they would not endorse me. But we built mutual respect for one another, and I neutralized what would often have been their strong opposition.

In order to survive, a legislator has to have collegiality. After all, the legislative experience is a group consensus process. I have said jokingly that I believe the best form of government is a benevolent dictatorship as long as I am the benevolent dictator, but it doesn't work that way.

I learned as a trial lawyer how to vigorously battle an opponent in trial and then go out and have coffee with him while the jury deliberated. To survive in the political arena, one must respect the process and the participants while disagreeing on the issues. In the end, one must be willing to accept a consensus, which often means getting a half bite of the apple, which is often better than getting no bite at all.

Lastly, and perhaps most importantly, a legislator needs to be well-rounded and not one-issue obsessed.

I was driven to run because of my passion for the protection of the unborn. I believe that ultimately the important issues of our time are not scientific, economic and technological, but rather moral and theological.

Over the years, I authored and passed many bills dealing with faith and family, but I have passed many other ones (more than five hundred, not counting amendments) as well. In the senate, I chaired seven committees, including criminal justice, education and judiciary, where I was the shepherd for a whole host of legislative initiatives. No one could accuse me of being a one-issue obsessionist.

IF YOU HAVE TO MAKE ENEMIES, THEN YOU MUST. SOMEONE ASKED ME ONE TIME HOW I MANAGED TO SURVIVE AS LONG AS I DID, AND I TOLD THEM THAT I MADE SURE I HAD MY SHARE OF ENEMIES.

I purposed to be identified as a well-rounded legislator. That is a trap many pro-life and pro-family legislators fall into. That's all they talk about, and whenever they rise to speak, it is another sermon that turns everyone else off.

This doesn't mean one is compromising on the issue. It does mean working together with people who disagree on an issue with the intent to discover common ground where you can help them.

Many politicians want to be all things to all people. By doing so, they stand for nothing and fall for everything. I learned that the dividends of making enemies on one side of an issue is the creation of an army of soldiers ready to fall under the bus for you on the other side of the issue.

Lastly, and this should go without saying, public office holders need to remember that they hold office day and night and should conduct themselves accordingly. Don't ever do anything inappropriate that will appear in the paper with your office title in the headline.

I have watched many political careers ruined, especially of those on our side, because they did or said something uncalled for at a time they were most vulnerable. If one is called to carry the pro-life, pro-family banner, one needs to live a clean life worthy of the calling.

I declined many invitations just because I knew who would be there and what they would be doing. I made certain I conducted myself with honor and integrity.

One powerful senator was destroyed by telling an inappropriate joke within earshot of the press. His career was over and he was forced to resign. In this time of camera phones, one needs to be more careful than ever. One post on Facebook can go around the world in eighty seconds.

Well, I was not only elected, but I survived seven years in the House. While we had not taken control from the majority party, we had increased our numbers by about fifty percent. We had turned up the heat on the pro-life issues enough that even members of the majority party were concerned about talking and voting right.

I was happy doing what I was doing and doing it where I was doing it. Little did I know that my political career was just about to really begin.

CHAPTER FOUR

ON TO THE SENATE

"We tremble not, we fear no ill, for they shall not overpower us."
-Martin Luther

Quite happy in my seat on the House of Representatives, I felt we had made progress and were heading in the right direction. On the other hand, the liberals were in tight control of the Senate, but hanging on by a thread with an inner party fight between the liberals and the conservatives.

While there were only eight members of the minority party, those members coupled with the conservatives in the majority party were close to being in control. A change in a couple of seats regardless of party could make a difference.

As pro-life conservatives in the House, we were facing a brick wall. We knew that any pro-life legislation we might pass out of the House would be dead on arrival in the Senate.

The senator from my district was part of the liberal party and not up for re-election in 1986. One morning my phone rang, and it was the press telling me that my senator was stepping down to run for statewide office. They were asking if I would run for the vacant seat.

I learned a long time ago in politics that when there is a knock at the door, you had better answer it before someone else does. Either make the call or get out of the phone booth.

WHEN THERE IS A KNOCK AT THE DOOR, YOU HAD BETTER ANSWER IT BEFORE SOMEONE ELSE DOES. EITHER MAKE THE CALL OR GET OUT OF THE PHONE BOOTH.

When I had awakened that morning, moving to the Senate had never crossed my mind, but now I was facing an instant decision. I had to say yes or no before they called the next person on their list, so with a deep breath, I said yes. I knew that if I could get elected, along with a couple of others, we could change the political landscape of Florida.

I had to drive a stake in the ground and let everyone know that if they wanted to get the minority party nomination, they had to beat me. I knew it was a risk. I was giving up a safe house seat to run for a highly contested senate seat in a two county district. The majority party had a considerable edge in registration, and the voters tilted toward the pro-choice position. However, a third of the district was totally my House district, so I felt that gave me an edge.

Once I announced my run, it became apparent that no one would challenge me for the nomination. The real question was who the majority party would put up and whether the candidate would have the backing of the liberal or conservative wing of the party.

A number of names were rumored to run in the majority party, and I shuddered at some, but initially no one took the bait. Finally and fortunately, the liberal wing came forth with a candidate. He was really a pretty conservative wealthy home builder who had previously supported me. In fact, his daughter and mine were the best of friends. But he was pledged to the liberal senator from Ft. Lauderdale, and that was all that mattered.

The minority party and the conservative wing of the majority party rallied behind me, and we had a barn burner of an election.

My opponent leveled the playing field by opening his account with a quarter of a million dollars from his own pocket. After all, money is the mother's milk of politics. Together we spent about $800,000, which broke records at the time. But now it is a low budget campaign. Just this last year, nearly five million dollars was spent in a two person senate primary.

Money is ruining the political process where large amounts

of money can be anonymously funneled into unidentified political action committees by special interest groups who want to buy access. In excess of a billion dollars was spent in the 2012 presidential race. This is absurd.

MONEY IS RUINING THE POLITICAL PROCESS WHERE LARGE AMOUNTS OF MONEY CAN BE ANONYMOUSLY FUNNELED INTO UNIDENTIFIED POLITICAL ACTION COMMITTEES BY SPECIAL INTEREST GROUPS.

Many of those PAC's are controlled by liberal billionaires who don't think or believe as we do on the social, family and moral issues. A large amount of their money is funneled to campaigns of candidates who are solidly pro-choice and who oppose the pro-life agenda.

At the end of the day, after a tough campaign, I won with a four-point margin. Together with the win of three other minority candidates and the conservatives of the majority party, we overthrew the designated liberal Senate president. This formed a coalition that put the minority party and the conservative wing of the majority party in charge. The liberals were now in the minority. While our party didn't occupy the president's podium, the minority party and the conservative wing of the majority party were in charge. The liberals were now in the minority and I was even named as vice-chairman of the Senate Judiciary Committee.

All of a sudden, the Senate changed from being liberal to conservative, and it was a difference of night and day. We kept chiseling away until, in 1994, we became the majority party. The same thing happened that year in the House, and in 1998, we elected a governor of our party.

It was also in 1994 when the Republicans took control of the U.S. House of Representatives and implemented the Contract With

America. Few people have stopped to analyze what happened, or more aptly put, few understood it.

The truth is that the Republicans strongly supported a pro-life plank in their platform along with evangelicals who had traditionally been loyal to the Democratic party. This began a significant party migration.

Public opinion was moving our way. We were able to make small strides in the fight against abortion.

In 1989, the United States Supreme Court handed down a decision in Webster v. Reproductive Health Services, upholding a Missouri law that imposed restrictions on the use of state funds, facilities, and employees in performing, assisting with, or counseling on abortions.

Thus, the Supreme Court in Webster allowed for states to legislate in an area that had previously been thought to be forbidden under Roe v. Wade. What that meant was that the court had backed off from Roe in a small amount and would allow states to adopt laws like Missouri's to further limit abortions.

The Governor called, and he wanted me to file three of four bills designed to conform Florida law to that of the State of Missouri that had been upheld by the United States Supreme Court. I agreed, and the special session was called.

The agenda included banning public financing and the use of public resources for abortions, expanding regulations for abortion clinics, requiring viability tests on the fetus of women who are at least twenty weeks pregnant and requiring physicians to tell women seeking abortions about the development of their fetuses.

Unfortunately, the special session ended with none of the bills being passed. All were procedurally killed in committee. Some if not all might have passed had they reached the floor of the House and Senate. At least there would have been a full and public debate.

This is a game many legislators play. They claim to support a position they don't want to vote on and then make sure they don't have to vote on it. I will speak more about that later regarding the legislation I filed defining marriage.

The special session was not only a disappointment to me, but one in which I received criticism from people who failed to understand basic ninth grade civics.

The bills I introduced were entitled "An Abortion Can Be Performed." People were all over me about it. I remember one night being asked to explain the bills to my church body at a Wednesday evening service.

People became angry with me for filing bills that permitted abortions and said I should be filing one bill to make all abortions under all circumstances illegal in Florida. Believe me, I would like to do nothing better, but my purpose was to restrict abortion as much as I could under the Webster case and not to pass something that would be declared unconstitutional under Roe.

Christians all too often tend to shoot their wounded and fail to understand the governmental process. To me, there is no excuse for an uninformed, non-voting and non-involved believer. In the most recent election in our county, there was a fifteen percent turnout and half who are eligible weren't even registered to vote. Maybe we deserve what we get. Studies show that Christian voting patterns are really no different than the public at large.

THERE IS NO EXCUSE FOR AN UNINFORMED, NON-VOTING AND NON-INVOLVED BELIEVER.

We made progress in the legislature, not so much in what we passed, but in the increasing of public awareness by getting pro-life bills to the floor for debate. As one who left the Senate, I believe that subsequent pro-life legislation passed was done so on the foundations we built.

For example, during the 2011 session, Florida lawmakers passed a battery of pro-life legislation, including a constitutional amendment that would ban public funding for abortion and prevent the state courts from interpreting a right to privacy to include abortion. Not all pro-life legislation became law, and some are subject to federal court interference, but just the public debate and passage is a refreshing turn from where I once was.

The Senate passed legislation which opts Florida out of having insurance policies covering elective abortion in the state health exchanges created by the national health care reform law (Obamacare).

The House also passed legislation which would require abortionists to perform an ultrasound for the review and benefit of a pregnant woman before an abortion. This was part of the state's informed consent laws. The law specifies that women may decline to view the ultrasound, but they must be offered the opportunity.

Another bill passed by the House strengthens parental notification requirements by making changes to the judicial bypass system. This bill prevents an individual from judge-shopping in other circuit courts in search of a judicial bypass and extends the time for a judge to consider a bypass request to three business days.

Also passed by the House was a law that would ban abortion once an unborn child has reached the age of viability. The law would also require all future clinic owners and operators to be physicians, not corporations.

All of this was accomplished in just one year. Florida has seen a surge of pro-life legislation in recent sessions and a dramatic increase of legislators and candidates who are proudly standing up in the fight for life of the unborn.

During the past five years, the number of abortions performed in Florida has fallen by nearly 20 percent. Pro-abortion critics contend that more women are reluctant to get the procedure, especially in light of recent laws that have made abortion more cumbersome.

The State of Florida reported 16,156 abortions in 1973, the year abortion was legalized by Roe v. Wade. The next year, the number fell slightly to 15,212. The number rose through the 1990's before peaking in 2006, when 95,586 reported abortions were performed. (Palm Beach Post August 13, 2012).

Oftentimes a woman in a crisis pregnancy isn't thinking rationally. When it is more difficult to get an abortion, there is more time for a woman to realize the consequences of her actions. Therefore, once these pieces of legislation are put into law, it actually has a positive impact in decreasing the number of abortions.

State lawmakers across America are considering legislation on many life and family related measures.

A long fight is behind us, but the battle is not won. We must press on.

CHAPTER FIVE

GROUND ZERO

"I say this to your shame. Is it so, that there is not among you one wise man who will be able to decide between his brethren, but brother goes to law with brother, and that before unbelievers?"
-1 Corinthians 6:5-6

In order to fight any enemy, one needs to know and understand the enemy. We fight cancer by studying cancer. Likewise, in order to fight abortion, we need to understand the roots of this crisis and how we unfortunately arrived where we are.

Abortion and the legal and social forces that allow the procedure are the enemy, and we have to commit ourselves in the cause of life to bring it to a halt.

Americans have always valued life, both in word and in deed. When it comes to saving a life, whether one lost at sea or one lost in the woods, we put no price cap on the cost of rescue. Or, put another way, human life is priceless.

More than two hundred years ago, brave men risked their lives, their fortunes and their sacred honor to publicly proclaim:

> *"We hold these truths to be self-evident, that all men are created equal, that they are endowed by their Creator with certain unalienable Rights, that among these are Life, Liberty and the pursuit of Happiness."*

These words are the very foundations for which this nation stands. Life is sacred. Life is basic. This Declaration of Independence opens with a proclamation that is "self evident" that "all" are created equal and endowed by their creator with these unalienable rights.

The declaration declares that we are "endowed", (that means divinely given), with the rights by our "Creator." There cannot be creation without a creator. In other words, the Declaration of Independence states that we (mortal men and women) do not re-create ourselves, but rather we are created by a higher power of creation and that is God.

Historically, Americans in general have always believed that life is sacred and that man cannot destroy what God has created. In the early history of the various states, few states had outlawed abortion or even saw a need to outlaw it. The sanctity of human life was just an inherent part of our Judeo-Christian culture.

However, as the underground abortion network began to appear, especially in urban areas, states began to recognize the need to restrict abortions. Various statutes against abortion began to appear in the 1820's.

In 1821, Connecticut passed a statute targeting apothecaries who sold poisons to women for purposes of abortion. Eight years later, New York made post-quickening abortions a felony and pre-quickening abortions a misdemeanor.

Therefore, it is sometimes argued that the early American abortion statutes were motivated not by ethical concerns about abortion, but by worry about the safety of the procedure. The criminalization movement accelerated during the 1860's, and by 1900, abortion was largely illegal in every state.

However, abortions continued to occur and increasingly became readily available. In the 1930's, licensed physicians performed an estimated 800,000 abortions a year.

I remember my mother telling me how her sister became pregnant while her husband was off fighting in the South Pacific during World War II. My mother took her to get an abortion. Sadly, after that procedure she was never able to get pregnant again, a consequence not uncommon post abortion.

Illegal abortions were often unsafe, sometimes resulting in death. In 1965, following the Supreme Court's decision in Griswold v. Connecticut declaring a constitutional right to contraceptives, the American College of Obstetricians and Gynecologists (ACOG) issued a medical bulletin accepting a recommendation from six years earlier which clarified that conception is implantation, not fertilization. This had the consequence of categorizing birth control methods that prevented implantation as contraceptives, not abortion implementers.

By the early 1970's, statutes regarding restricting abortion existed in all fifty states. Thirty states made it totally illegal and twenty made it legal only in certain specified situations, such as rape and incest.

Each state made its own decision, and that is important to note since all rights not specifically designated to the federal government are specifically reserved for the various states under the federal constitution. That is a very important fact to remember as one marches down contemporary history regarding abortion in America.

Then, in 1973, the bomb dropped and it became ground zero for "abortionazia" in America. The case, *Roe v. Wade,* originating in Dallas, Texas was argued in 1971 and reargued in 1972 before a decision was finally handed down from the Supreme Court in January of 1973. Decided simultaneously with a companion case, Doe v. Bolton, the Court ruled that a right to privacy under the due process clause of the 14th Amendment extended to a woman's decision to have an abortion,

Thus in one ruling, the Court deemed abortion a fundamental right under the United States Constitution, thereby subjecting all laws attempting to restrict it to the standard of strict scrutiny. In other words, by so ruling the court cast aside (7-2) the laws of all states regarding abortion and usurped to the province of the federal government the right to control abortion.

By legalizing abortion, the court defied the unalienable right to life and allowed the most marginalized and voiceless group in America to be slaughtered in the womb.

I believe Roe to be one of the two most insidious, socially divisive and morally destructive decisions ever in the history of

American judicature. The other would be the Dred Scott case. It represents the ultimate in judicial activism. In other words, the court chose a solution and looked for law to wrap it in. Roe is the epitome of judicial engineering and reeks of a violation of the separation of powers clause in the constitution.

I BELIEVE ROE TO BE ONE OF THE TWO MOST INSIDIOUS, SOCIALLY DIVISIVE AND MORALLY DESTRUCTIVE DECISIONS EVER IN THE HISTORY OF AMERICAN JUDICATURE.

Abortion is nothing less than fetal homicide. I have personally witnessed a suction abortion and cringed as I saw tiny little body parts extracted and discarded. That day, I vowed to do everything in my power to stop this terrible practice.

The reaction to Roe was divisive and reactionary. Conservatives believed that they had been ambushed and the state's rights rug had been pulled out from under them.

Liberals felt they had scored a much celebrated victory. It should be noted that the decision was nearly simultaneous with the passage of the Equal Rights Amendment. It was passed by Congress and certified to the states for ratification, where it failed to be ratified by the necessary number of states. The feminists were on a roll.

The mention of Roe v. Wade immediately provoked a verbal, if not ugly, battleground. Few other decisions handed down by the U.S. Supreme Court have exerted such far-reaching ramifications and generated so much controversy as Roe.

Roe also gave evidence of a deeply divided court. Dissenting Justices White and Rehnquist voiced their disgust, calling the court's decision an "exercise of raw judicial power . . .(with no Constitutional support). The court simply fashions and announces a new constitutional right for pregnant mothers . . . ."

Those of the more liberal camp, such as Justice Blackmun,

continued to make their voices heard, praising Roe as "essential to women's equality and reproductive freedom."

Immediately states began to pass abortion restrictive laws which they thought could stand muster under Roe. Some did and some did not. Most were struck down by lower federal courts.

Many states chose to limit certain rights to an abortion. Some of the laws that spun off the case dealt with requiring parental consent to obtain an abortion for minors, spousal consent laws, laws barring state funding for abortions, mandated waiting periods, requirements that certain informational pamphlets be read before proceeding with the abortion, and many more.

At one time or another most all of these found their way into bills in the Florida legislature. Those able to make it out of committee and onto the floor agenda were debated thoroughly on the floors of the House and the Senate.

While we knew there were insufficient votes to pass these bills at the time, it gave us a great forum to educate people about the evils and horrors of abortion. It also caused the press and media to solidify its already abortion leaning positions. I was raked over the coals numerous times, even being called a Neanderthal on one occasion.

Legislation at the national level occurred in September 1976, when the "Hyde Amendment," which essentially banned federal funding for abortions, was enacted. Gone, too, were abortions in overseas military hospitals, and international family-planning clinics could no longer receive federal aid.

Some of the most vicious and nationally focused consent hearings followed in the U.S. Senate on future Supreme Court nominees. The prime focus was whether or not a proposed justice would be on one side or the other in efforts to overturn Roe. One needs to only recall Clarence Thomas who was confirmed and Robert Bork who was not. The liberal wing felt Bork might be the turning vote. When Ronald Reagan became President, he established a litmus test for appointees to the court.

In a bit of legal irony, it should be noted that by the time the court considered the matter, Norma McCorvey (aka Jane Roe) had given birth, which under "normal rules of the court," would have rendered the lawsuit moot.

In a strange twist of history, McCorvey, after giving birth and following her conversion to Christianity, came down on the side of the pro-life movement.

Roe was about more than abortion. It had massive social ramifications, as we will see in the next chapter. It also established a precedent for more judicial activism by courts in cases on all kinds of matters.

This flies in the face of the separation of powers clause. To this day, between judicial activism at the federal level and the abuse of executive orders in the White House, it has significantly reduced the power of the legislative branch in all areas of governance.

Roe not only opened the doors to wholesale abortion in America, but also forever changed the political and social landscape of our land.

CHAPTER SIX

THE SOCIAL FALL OUT

"What then shall I do when God rises up? When He punishes, how shall I answer Him? Did not He who made me in the womb make them? Did not the same One fashion us in the womb?"

Job 31:14-15

Roe was the capstone on a sexual revolution which began with the pill in the 1950's. When the medical community determined that pregnancy was not decided by fertilization but rather by implantation in the wall of the uterus, it meant that a hormone that precluded implantation of the fertilized egg was not legally considered to be an abortion. Therefore, dispensing of the pill circumvented abortion statutes.

This caused a cascade of epochal consequences. Just to tally a few of the big-ticket items:

- uncoupled sex from reproduction
- caused people to have sex earlier and marry later
- increased divorce, cohabitation, and illegitimacy
- revolutionized the economic role of women
- imploded the fertility rate
- set the modern welfare state on the course to insolvency

The sexual revolution unleashed by contraceptive sex, says Mary Eberstadt, (The Pill Perplex, July 23, 2012 Weekly Standard) rivals the Communist revolution in terms of its influence on the world in the 20th century.

The sexual revolution has been a primary factor in the weakening of the marriage culture over the last half-century. The abandonment of marriage, either by cohabitation or through divorce has, by every measure, stunted and harmed American children, women and our society as a whole.

Sex, Eberstadt points out, has been "stripped of moral stigmas and codes and reduced to a kind of hygienic recreation."

Under Roe, abortion became the ultimate method of contraception. It has been referred to as the "final solution." If everything else fails, abortion is the ultimate way to prevent pregnancy, and it is one hundred percent effective.

I find it strange to hear abortion referred to as the final solution. As I recall, The Final Solution was Nazi Germany's plan and execution of the systematic genocide of European Jews during World War II, resulting in the most deadly phase of the Holocaust. The Nazis frequently used euphemistic language to disguise the true nature of their crimes. They used the term, "Final Solution" to refer to their plan to annihilate the Jewish people.

I see a parallel here. Don't you? Genocide is genocide!

The sexual revolution isn't just about sex. The chain reaction it set off has affected pornography and divorce and gender roles. It has shaped the modern college experience. The sexual revolution has altered ideas about child rearing and has placed a different perspective on marriage.

Please, don't misunderstand me. I am not suggesting that contraceptives used within marriage for family planning is wrong. I am suggesting that abortion and contraceptives which lead to unleashed recreational sex is wrong and has revolutionized sexual behavior in America. Abortion under any circumstances other than to save the life of the mother is always wrong, regardless of the circumstances giving rise to the conception.

As I write this book, I read in this morning's paper that the fourth in line to be King of England was photographed naked in a Las Vegas hotel after playing a game of strip billiards. Is that not a fallout of the sexual revolution?

Abortion has cheapened sex and has also cheapened life. National morality has hit an all time low. The cheapening of life has more ramifications than the tentacles of an octopus.

Recently, a homeless man in our city was senselessly beaten to death, and I received an e-mail that someone had shot eleven people near the Empire State Building in New York. Oftentimes, gangs require a prospective member to shoot someone or to father a child in order to be admitted to their gang.

While many disagree with me, I believe that the slaughter of more than fifty million babies in this country since Roe has so cheapened human life that these kinds of incidents continue to occur more frequently.

I might also say that the emergence of violent video games has contributed to this violent and aggressive behavior as well. When I was in the Senate, I introduced legislation to restrict some types of violent video games being sold to or watched by minors. The bill created a fire storm and became a lobbyist relief act as people were retained by very profitable firms to defeat the legislation.

Numerous studies show that video games, especially ones with violent content, make teens more aggressive. This makes the video game industry a powerful force in many adolescent lives.

A study conducted by Gentile, Lynch, Linder & Walsh (Gentile, D. A., Lynch, P., Linder, J. & Walsh, D. (2004) on The Effects of Violent Video Game Habits on Adolescent Hostility, Aggressive Behaviors, and School Performance published in the Journal of Adolescence, 27, 5-22.) states that "adolescent girls played video games for an average of 5 hours a week, whereas boys averaged 13 hours a week". The authors also stated that teens who play violent video games for extended periods of time:

- Tend to be more aggressive
- Are more prone to confrontation with their teachers
- May engage in fights with their peers

The interactive quality of video games differs from passively viewing television or movies because it allows players to become active participants in the game's script. Players benefit from engaging in acts of violence and are then able to move to the game's next level.

Gentile & Anderson state that playing video games may increase aggressive behavior because violent acts are continually repeated throughout the video game. This method of repetition has long been considered an effective teaching method in reinforcing learning patterns.

Video games also encourage players to identify with and role-play their favorite characters. This is referred to as a "first-person" video game because players are able to make decisions affecting the actions of the character they are imitating. After a limited amount of time playing a violent video game, a player can "automatically prime aggressive thoughts."

The researchers concluded that players who had prior experience playing violent video games responded with an increased level of aggression when they encountered confrontation (Bushman, B. & Anderson, C. (2002). Violent Video Games and Hostile Expectations: A Test of the General Aggression Model. Personality and Social Psychology Bulletin, 28, 1679-1686).

In a Joint Statement (2000) before the Congressional Public Health Summit, a number of American medical associations -- the American Medical Association, American Academy of Pediatrics, American Psychological Association, American Academy of Family Physicians and American Academy of Child & Adolescent Psychiatry -- cautioned parents about violence in the media and its negative effect on children.

Their report states that exposure to violent media can elevate aggressive feelings and thoughts, especially in children. These effects of aggressive behavior can be long-term. Although fewer studies have been conducted on interactive video games, evidence suggests that playing violent video games may have a more dramatic influence on the behavior of children and adolescents (Joint Statement on the Impact of Entertainment Violence on Children: Congressional Public Health Summit. July 26, 2000).

This is just another example of the cheapening of life. What children learn to do in animation, they are more inclined to do in reality.

THIS IS JUST ANOTHER EXAMPLE OF THE CHEAPENING OF LIFE. WHAT CHILDREN LEARN TO DO IN ANIMATION, THEY ARE MORE INCLINED TO DO IN REALITY.

Sex was once reserved for marriage. It was not only the God given way for people to reproduce and replace themselves, but it was the most intimate and loving of all human relationships. When two become one in the marriage bed, it is more than a physical relationship. It is sacred. It is wonderful. It is marriage.

I have been married to the wonderful bride God gave me forty six years ago, and I vividly remember our wedding night as if it were last night. I feel towards her in a way I could feel for no other woman. She is all mine, and I am all hers.

Sex has not only given us three wonderful children, but it has sustained an intimate relationship that cannot be described in words. Yes, it is a physical relationship, a joining of two bodies into one, but it is so much more.

But the sexual revolution and abortion have traded sacred sex for recreational sex. For many, it is now the equivalent to kissing on the first date. No sex, no second date.

The Biblical admonition requiring sexual faithfulness in marriage (Thou shalt not commit adultery) seems to many people in this post-modern era to be needlessly restrictive. Why not allow interchangeability with men and women enjoying each other freely? We have the biological equipment for such practices.

But sex transcends biology as it intertwines with romantic love and the need for stable families. If we break this one law to gain the freedom of sexual experimentation, we lose the long term benefits of intimacy that marriage is intended to provide.

Education has now stepped in and acquiesced to the fact that if children are going to have sex, it should at least be safe sex. So, they have begun teaching about it in grades far too low for my comfort.

Genital models and contraception devices are displayed and children are taught how to use them. Some are even dispensed from school health clinics. Many college dorms now have vending machines to dispense condoms and "morning after" pills.

Has this worked? Of course, it hasn't. Rather than discouraging sex, it has actually promoted it, and the idea of prevention of disease has not worked either.

Sexually transmitted diseases (STD's) are escalating, and nearly forty percent of babies born in the United States are delivered by unwed mothers, according to data released by the National Center for Health Statistics.

The 1.7 million out-of-wedlock births of 4.3 million total births marked a more than 25 percent jump from five years before. The figure for unwed births in the African-American community is 70 percent.

This creates an incredible future social and financially unfunded public liability. Who is going to pay the bill?

Out-of-wedlock babies are usually denied the opportunity to live and be reared in a more traditional family, and more than likely, they will grow up lacking a male role model to help shape them for adulthood.

Some say abortion is good because it keeps down child abuse of children who would otherwise be reared in a hostile environment.

THE CHILD ABUSE RATE IN THE UNITED STATES IS NOW ALMOST SIX TIMES HIGHER THAN IT WAS IN 1972,

THE YEAR BEFORE THE SUPREME COURT'S ROE V. WADE DECISION.

The child abuse rate in the United States is now almost six times higher than it was in 1972, the year before the Supreme Court's Roe v. Wade decision.

Abortion propagandist Larry Lader ("The Abortion Revolution." The Humanist, May/June 1973, page 4.) wrote: "The impact of the abortion revolution may be too vast to assess immediately. It should usher in an era when every child will be wanted, loved, and properly cared for; when the incidence of infanticides and battered children should be sharply reduced."

Pro-abortionists are perhaps even worse forecasters of social trends than the well-known mediums who grace the covers of those sensational supermarket tabloids.

This is because the pro-abortionists have a vested interest in painting a rosy picture of the future for public consumption. Their predictions are not based upon any studies or facts, but instead on unsupported propaganda that's intended to prop up their industry.

The irony in abortionists claiming that abortion will decrease child abuse is glaringly obvious. After all, abortion itself is the greatest child abuse. Every day in this country, we burn, cut to pieces, and decapitate a living preborn child every five seconds during working hours.

The abortionists, of course, do not really put the abuse of born children very high on their agenda. Their phony hand-wringing and histrionics have one purpose and one purpose only. That is to keep their precious abortion 'right' freely and easily available.

Pro-abortionists insist that abortion is a good thing for society, because it will simply eliminate any children that might, at some point in the future, suffer at the hands of abusive adults. The increasing numbers of tiny broken and battered bodies in this country are mute, but there is powerful evidence to the contrary.

The National Abortion Rights Action League stated:

"A policy that makes contraception and abortion freely available will greatly reduce the number of unwanted

children, and thereby curb the tragic rise of child abuse in our country ... Legal abortion will decrease the number of unwanted children, battered children, child abuse cases, and possibly subsequent delinquency, drug addiction, and a host of social ills believed to be associated with neglectful parenthood."

(National Abortion Rights Action League. A Speaker's and Debater's Notebook, June 1978, pages 7 and 8.)

Even if a child is unwanted, battered and lives a miserable life, at least he or she has a chance to improve his or her life after leaving home. Anyone who asserts that the battered child would rather die than be abused is supremely arrogant. After all, everyone knows the stories of people who have overcome the most extreme adversity to find happiness. Those who believe that children would rather be aborted than abused have obviously never spoken to adults who were abused as children.

This can be a good point for a pro-life debater to make before an audience. The pro-lifer might ask those people in the audience who were abused to raise their hands, and then ask those who would rather have died at the hands of an abortionist to stand up and explain why.

Pornography cannot be totally disassociated with abortion. With the rise of cable and satellite television, as well as strip clubs to arouse sexual appetites, it has further cheapened sex. These influences have made an evening recreational escapade much akin to a game of racquetball, and if you lose, abortion is always there to erase the debt.

How ironic that those who scream for "women's rights" are not totally adamant against pornography. I can think of nothing that more demeans the status of women than pornography, which reduces the naked body to a sex symbol.

I remember one day standing with the leader of the women's

rights movement along with a member of the Senate as we were waiting for our cars. When the leader of the women's right movement pulled up, I couldn't help but notice the porno magazines on the back seat. When she saw that I had noticed, she said that she collected those for her husband! Somehow that didn't seem to add up, but maybe her marriage was different from mine.

I remain amazed at the women I know who have confessed to having had an abortion, and few are in retrospect glad that they had one. If there have been over fifty million abortions since Roe, that means there are fifty million or so post abortion women.

As I was working on this book, our housekeeper asked what I was doing, so I told her. She tearfully said she had experienced four abortions. She is now a happily married lady with two adult children whom she only recently told about her past. She is also an ardent pro-life supporter. The following is her story that she allowed me to use:

> *My name is Amy and this is my story. In my teen years, I found myself looking for love in all the wrong places. At the age of seventeen, I found out I was pregnant. After talking it over with my parents and his parents, I decided to get an abortion. After all, this was not what I had planned at that age. Having a baby then would have been inconvenient.*
>
> *I went to the local abortion clinic and I received counseling from them that, "This would be the best decision, after all at this point it is just a piece of tissue". I agreed and had the procedure done. I left there feeling lonely, but went on with my life as usual. I tried not to think about my abortion. I don't remember having many emotions about it. Life goes on.*
>
> *A year and a half later, I found myself in the same situation, pregnant, and not ready to accept responsibility again. So, I thought about abortion again. It's just a piece*

of tissue, right? Life goes on, no remorse or feelings about it.

I am very sad to say that this happened two more times. Yes, I had a total of four abortions. I read a quote that I thought really applied to my situation:

'We are free up to the point of choice, and then the choice controls the chooser.'.

WE ARE FREE UP TO THE POINT OF CHOICE, AND THEN THE CHOICE CONTROLS THE CHOOSER.

And that is exactly what I felt. The choice had controlled me. At this point, I was sad I had made these decisions, but I still had no understanding as to what had really happened.

Fast forward ten years when I fell in love with Jesus and gave my life to Him. Things started to change in my heart and God began working in my life. I was invited to attend a three-day weekend retreat. It was there where I met His redemption because of His bloody cross, and all of a sudden the Holy Spirit revealed to me that the four abortions were not tissues ...but were four lives. I was devastated with deep anguish, and so ashamed. I had a Godly sorrow and was deeply hurt that I had done that.

There God met me with grace, mercy, forgiveness and most of all- love. All weekend, He was restoring me to the uttermost. God brought an awareness to my life that was much needed. In the Bible, Hosea 4:6 says, "My people are destroyed for lack of knowledge."

And, really, that is what had happened to me! My four children were destroyed because of my lack of knowledge as to what an abortion was really about. They had told me at the abortion clinic that it was only tissue and there would be no side effects. All I knew was that I no longer had to deal with the abortions. I had felt at that time, my life was not to be inconvenienced, or so I thought.

After God had revealed Himself to me and the truth was exposed, I would find myself crying, sadly thinking about how old they would be, and what they looked like. It was in my thoughts a lot. Finally, I came to the point where I began to realize that the scripture Romans 8:28 was for me. It says, "And we know that God causes everything to work together for good to those who love Him and are called according to their purpose for them."

I was asked to do a talk while I was at this three-day retreat. When I began to write out my talk, I felt the Lord wanted me to reveal the story about my abortions. I was not ready to speak that out loud to anyone. I had dealt with it, but no one else needed to know as far as I was concerned. I felt I would be judged, talked about, or possibly cast aside.

But, I submitted to God. I gave my testimony, and thirty of the thirty-eight women present came to me at the retreat and said: "Me, too." Some had never admitted it before and had never told anyone before that retreat. They were longing to be set free also. I shared with them how God set me free supernaturally from what had happened in the natural.

I told God I would use this to share the truth with others. He started giving me opportunities to share with others on an individual basis, as I felt led. It was amazing how God was using this horrible thing to help others be set free from the lies we were all told. We thought there were no side effects in having an abortion.

I was later asked to talk to a group of teenagers. A year after that teen event, I got a phone call from a young girl who had heard my story. She told me about a girl at her work who was scheduled to have an abortion the next day.

She wanted me to talk to her and to share my testimony.

I called my prayer partner to join me, and we shared the word of God and the truth of what the side effects would really be. We wanted her to know that it was truly a baby. A year and a half later, I received an invitation for a 1st year birthday party to celebrate the life of "Meadow." The girl did not have an abortion and now her daughter was a year old! The mother wanted to thank us for speaking the truth and praying for her and her boyfriend to have a change of heart about the abortion.

What a gift that was to see that little girl in person as a direct result of being bold, speaking the truth, and how that influenced their decision to give birth. She knew it was not merely a tissue growing inside her, but was a living person made in the image of God.

Guilt and shame always have more power when it's kept in secret.

GUILT AND SHAME HAVE MORE POWER WHEN KEPT IN SECRET.

I later attended a Pat Layton conference called, "Imagine Me Set Free." I told God if there is anything else I need to be free from, let's do it! I didn't want to hold back anything. I wanted to be used more to help people understand what was happening to them after their abortion and how to be set free. But, I had never even told my own children how many abortions I had experienced.

During that weekend conference, God allowed me to have an opportunity to share my story with my children. I told them I was not proud of my abortions, but it is a story of God's redeeming power!!

I learned the hard way that abortion did affect me. It effected me mentally, emotionally and physically. It is not a piece of tissue. It is a life, made in the image of God.

I am so grateful for the cross. Jesus, paid it all, all to Him I owe. Sin had left a crimson stain. But, He washed it white as snow. Now I am free. I am truly free, at last!

In conclusion, there is another social consequence of abortion. The economic fallout cannot be ignored, and it is now coming back as a serious blow to our nation's economy.

The fifty-three million babies who have been aborted are neither producing nor consuming. They are also not paying taxes. We have wiped out a generation. The loss of these Americans and the onset of senior status for the baby boomers have put Social Security totally out of balance. Just recently, Social Security began paying out more than it takes in, and that trend will only accelerate.

The bottom line is that Roe forever changed the social landscape of American society, and it must be reversed.

CHAPTER SEVEN

LIFE IS SACRED

"I praise you, for I am fearfully and wonderfully made. Wonderful are your works; my soul knows it very well. My frame was not hidden from you, when I was being made in secret, intricately woven in the depths of the earth."

Psalm 139:14-15

It is difficult to fathom the depth and depravity of abortion without understanding the glory of creation from both a Biblical and scientific perspective.

Without reservation, I am a born again Bible believing Christian who believes that the Bible is true from Genesis to Revelation! The Word of God is reliable, dependable and true. It is a compass for all the pathways of life.

THE WORD OF GOD IS RELIABLE, DEPENDABLE AND TRUE. IT IS A COMPASS FOR ALL THE PATHWAYS OF LIFE.

The Bible doesn't call abortion by that term, but the Bible does address the issue. Consider these verses:

> *"Then the word of the LORD came to me, saying: "Before I formed you in the womb I knew you; before you were born I sanctified you; I ordained you a prophet to the nations."*
>
> *Jeremiah 1:4-5*

This passage declares that God Himself said that He "formed" and He "knew" the baby "in the womb... before" the baby was "born."

> *"What then shall I do when God rises up? When He punishes, how shall I answer Him? Did not He who made me*

*in the womb make them? Did not the same One fashion
us in the womb?"*

Job 31:14-15

This passage affirms that "God... made" the baby "in the womb."

*"For You formed my inward parts; You covered me in my
mother's womb. I will praise You, for I am fearfully and
wonderfully made; marvelous are Your works, and that
my soul knows very well."*

Psalm 139:13-14

The "You" in this passage of course refers to God, who "formed"
the baby's "inward parts."

Luke 1:15 states that John the Baptist will be "filled with the
Holy Spirit, even from his mother's womb." This means that the
baby in the womb has a soul for the Holy Spirit to fill.

Abortion activists often attempt heroic acrobatics with logic to
try to dismiss these Bible verses which indicate that abortion kills
babies whom God "formed,""sanctified" and "made" in the womb
and in whom the Holy Spirit may already reside. Therefore, abortion is a murderous rebellion against God.

The "choice" pregnant women have is between keeping or
giving up their babies for adoption. There is no choice given to
murder the "wonderfully made marvelous ... works" of God. It is
unconscionable that 1.3 million unborn and even born babies are
murdered annually in America. To put this atrocity into perspective,
1.3 million is even more than the number of Jews the Nazis gassed
annually during the Holocaust. (GodVoter.org)

The fact that abortions are so common in America today does
not make them right. To the contrary, it only increases the scale of
the crime and rebellion against God.

In Genesis, we learn that God created man in His own image,
and nowhere does it say that it applied only to Serial Number One
(Adam). It applies to every person ever made and to all those who

will be made in the future. And what's more, each and every one of them is unique.

> *"The Lord said, 'Let us make man in our image, in our likeness, and let them rule over the fish of the sea and the birds of the air, over the livestock, over all the earth, and over all the creatures that move along the ground.' So God created man in his own image, in the image of God he created him; male and female he created them."*
> *Genesis 1:26,27*

We have before us a profound and awesome truth that everyone needs to understand. God created the first man and woman in His own image! Think of it! God made man to be like Him! Truly, man is the most important creature among all the creatures that God made. Only man was created in the image of God.

Now then, what does the Word of God mean when it says: *"God created man in His own image"*?

In the second chapter of Genesis, Scripture says:

> *"The Lord God formed the man from the dust of the ground and breathed into his nostrils the breath of life, and the man became a living being (soul)."*
> *Genesis 2:7*

We notice in this verse that when God created the first man, He created him with two elements: a body and a soul. Man is not merely a physical being. He has a body and a soul.

God created man in two steps. Look again to what the Scriptures say, in the first portion of this verse that first, *"The Lord God formed the man from the dust of the ground."* Second, God *"breathed into his nostrils the breath of life, and the man became a living soul."* Some abortionists believe that until the baby takes a breath, it is not a living soul. This is both obviously false and contrary to Scripture.

From this Scripture, we learn that when God created man, He first formed a body. Why did God make the body first? He made the body first because it would be the dwelling place into which He would place man's soul.

Yes, we are body and soul. One is temporary and the other eternal.

"To You, Oh Lord, I lift up my soul."
Psalm 25:1

Do you know that your body is your house? It is the temporary "tent" in which "the real you" (your soul) lives. That is what the Scriptures teach, saying, "The body we have on earth is like a tent." (2 Corinthians 5:1) God created the human body for the soul to dwell in.

Why did God create us? The short answer to this profound question is that He created us "for His pleasure." Revelation 4:11 says, "You are worthy, our Lord and God, to receive glory and honor and power, for You created all things, and by Your will they were created and have their being."

Colossians 1:16 reiterates the point that "All things were created by Him and for Him." Being created for God's pleasure does not mean humanity was made to entertain God or provide Him with amusement. God is a creative Being and it gives Him pleasure to create. God is a personal Being and it gives Him pleasure to have a genuine relationship with His created beings.

Being made in the image and likeness of God (Genesis 1:27), human beings have the ability to know God and therefore love Him, worship Him, serve Him, and fellowship with Him.

You and I were created to bring great joy to God:

"According as He hath chosen us in Him before the foundation of the world, that we should be holy and without blame before Him in love: Having predestinated us unto the adoption of children by Jesus Christ to Himself, according to the good pleasure of His will."
Ephesians 1:4-5

Wow! Not only did God create us, but He also had uniquely

designed us before the formation of the world.

God also made us unique not only to fellowship and worship with Him, but to minister to others. God created Jeremiah to share God's message with others; in the same way, He created you and me to share His love and grace with those around us.

> *"Before I formed you in the womb I knew you, before you were born I set you apart; I appointed you as a prophet to the nations."*
> *Jeremiah 1:5*

Perhaps the most quoted scripture on this subject comes from Psalm 139:13-14:

> *"For you created my inmost being; You knit me together in my mother's womb. I praise You because I am fearfully and wonderfully made; Your works are wonderful, I know that full well."*

Imagine that! The Bible says you and I were prescribed before birth. God knew what we would look like. He chose our every characteristic. That means we are unique. There is only one you. There is no one on earth now or who has ever lived or who will ever live in the future exactly like you. We are wonderfully personal and complex.

I don't believe that anyone was ever created by accident, regardless of the manner of persons who are a part of the conception. I know something about physiology, but I also understand theology. Creation is a divine event orchestrated by God in fulfillment of a plan He has designed long ago.

Traditional marriage ceremonies often end with the admonishment, "What therefore God hath joined together, let not man put asunder." It comes from Mark 10:9 and gives reference to the fact that marriage is one of the sacraments of the church joined by God and, therefore, should not be separated by man.

I think that scripture applies equally to conception. If God brought it together, it would be wrong for man to tear it apart.

What God is saying to us is that human life is sacred. He gave it, and it has enormous worth. He wants us to respect human life because it is in the image of Himself. Whoever commits the sacrilege of murder must be punished.

The deepest human relationship possible is marriage. God gave it to satisfy the essential loneliness in the heart of every person. To spread among a variety of people what is meant to be reserved for marriage only devalues and destroys that relationship.

I believe that God wants us to save sex and intimacy for its rightful place in marriage.

So the Bible is very compelling about God's role in conception, but so also is the biological process so unique and so intricate that only a divine creator could bring it about.

There are accidental parents, but no accidental children. God created every one of them and all for a distinct purpose and mission in life.

I find it interesting that insurance policies, various legal documents and the like refer to "ACTS OF GOD," but somehow many fail to realize that the creation of human life is also an act of God. He alone created life and He does it at conception.

Therefore, how do you think God feels when one of His children (that He has a planned destiny for) is taken from Him?

An amazing series of events take place in a short period of time when a woman is pregnant. The Mayo Clinic has described the incredible development process:

THE FIRST TRIMESTER

Fetal development begins soon after conception, and from that point the baby grows and develops during the first trimester.
Weeks 1 and 2: Getting ready

It might seem strange, but the woman is not actually pregnant the first week or two of the time allotted to the pregnancy. Yes, you read that correctly!

Conception typically occurs about two weeks after a woman's period begins. To calculate the due date, the health care provider will count ahead 40 weeks from the start of her last period. This means that the period is counted as part of her pregnancy even though she was not pregnant at the time.

Week 3: Fertilization

Fertilization and implantation: The sperm and egg unite in one of the woman's fallopian tubes to form a one-celled entity called a zygote. If more than one egg is released and fertilized, she may have multiple zygotes.

The zygote has 46 chromosomes, 23 from the female and 23 from the male. These chromosomes will help determine the baby's sex, traits such as eye and hair color, and, to some extent, personality and intelligence.

Soon after fertilization, the zygote travels down the fallopian tube toward the uterus. At the same time, it will begin dividing rapidly to form a cluster of cells resembling a tiny raspberry. The inner group of cells will become the embryo.

Week 4: Implantation

By the time it reaches the uterus, the rapidly dividing ball of cells, now known as a blastocyst, has separated into two sections. The inner group of cells will become the embryo. The outer group will become the cells that nourish and protect it. On contact, it will burrow into the uterine wall for nourishment. This process is called implantation. The placenta, which will nourish the baby throughout the pregnancy, also begins to form.

Week 5: The embryonic period begins

The fifth week of pregnancy, or the third week after conception, marks the beginning of the embryonic period. This is when the baby's brain, spinal cord, heart and other organs begin to form.

The embryo is now made of three layers. The top layer, the ectoderm, will give rise to the baby's outermost layer of skin, central and peripheral nervous systems, eyes, inner ear, and many connective tissues.

The baby's heart and a primitive circulatory system will form in the middle layer of cells, the mesoderm. This layer of cells will also serve as the foundation for the baby's bones, muscles, kidneys and much of the reproductive system.

The inner layer of cells, the endoderm, will become a simple tube lined with mucous membranes. The baby's lungs, intestines and bladder will develop here.

By the end of this week, the baby is likely about the size of the tip of a pen.

Week 6: The neural tube closes

Growth is rapid this week. Just four weeks after conception, the neural tube along your baby's back is closing and the baby's heart is pumping blood.

Basic facial features will begin to appear, including passageways that will make up the inner ear and arches that will contribute to the jaw. The baby's body begins to take on a C-shaped curvature. Small buds will soon become arms and legs.

Week 7: Baby's head develops

Seven weeks into the pregnancy, or five weeks after conception, the baby's brain and face are rapidly developing. Tiny nostrils become visible, and the eye lenses begin to form. The arm buds that sprouted last week now take on the shape of paddles.

By the end of this week, the baby might be a little bigger than the top of a pencil eraser.

Week 8: Baby's eyes are visible

Eight weeks into the pregnancy, the baby's arms and legs are growing longer, and fingers have begun to form. The shell-shaped parts of the baby's ears also are forming, and the baby's eyes are visible. The upper lip and nose have formed. The trunk of the baby's body is beginning to straighten.

By the end of this week, the baby might be about 1/2 inch (11 to 14 millimeters) long.

Week 9: Baby's toes form

In the ninth week of pregnancy, or seven weeks after conception, the baby's arms grow, develop bones and bend at the elbows. Toes form, and the baby's eyelids and ears continue developing.

By the end of this week, the baby might be about 3/4 inch (18 to 22 millimeters) long.

Week 10: Baby's neck begins to develop

By the 10th week of pregnancy, or eight weeks after conception, the baby's head has become more round. The neck begins to develop, and the baby's eyelids begin to close to protect his or her developing eyes.

Week 11: Baby's genitals develop

At the beginning of the 11th week of pregnancy, the baby's head still makes up about half of its length. However, the baby's body is about to catch up, growing rapidly in the coming weeks.

This week the baby's eyes are widely separated, the eyelids fused and the ears are now set. Red blood cells are beginning to form in the baby's liver. By the end of this week, the baby's external genitalia will start developing into a penis or clitoris and labia majora.

By now the baby might measure about 2 inches (50 millimeters) long from crown to rump and weigh almost 1/3 ounce (8 grams).

Week 12: Baby's fingernails develop

Twelve weeks into the pregnancy, the baby is developing fingernails. The baby's face now has a human profile.

Is that amazing or what? Back on day 22, the heart began to beat with its own blood, often a blood type different than the mother's.

Time Magazine recently had a cover story entitled: "How the First Nine Months Shape the Rest of Your Life." And they were not referring to the first nine months after birth. The article spoke of how much life after birth is related to what happens between conception and birth:

> *But there's another powerful source of influence you may not have considered: your life as a fetus. The nutrition you received in the womb; the pollutants, drugs and infections you were exposed to during gestation; your mother's health and state of mind while she was pregnant with you, all these factors shaped you as a baby and continue to affect you to this day.*
>
> *This is the provocative contention of a field known as fetal origins, whose pioneers assert that the nine months of gestation constitute the most consequential period of our lives, permanently influencing the wiring of the brain and the functioning of organs such as the heart, liver and pancreas. In the literature on the subject, which has exploded over the past 10 years, you can find references to the fetal origins of cancer, cardiovascular disease, allergies, asthma, hypertension, diabetes, obesity, mental illness. At the farthest edge of fetal-origins research, scientists are exploring the possibility that intrauterine conditions influence not only our physical health but also our intelligence, temperament, even our sanity. (Time Magazine October 4, 2010 Cover Story)*

Lewis Thomas, (The Medusa and the Snail, Viking Press, 1979, 155-57) mused about why people made such a fuss over the first test tube baby in England. The true miracle, he affirms, "is the common union of a sperm and egg in a process that ultimately produces a human being. The mere existence of that cell should be one of the greatest astonishments of the earth. People ought to be walking around all day, all through their waking hours, calling to each other in endless wonderment, talking of nothing except that cell."

One of the greatest works on the human body is *Fearfully and Wonderfully Made* by Dr. Paul Brand and Phillip Yancey (Zondervan 1980). In this book, they describe the conception and gestation process:

> Over nine months these cells divide up functions in exquisite ways. Billions of blood cells appear, millions of rods and cones – in all, up to one hundred million cells form from a single fertilized ovum. And finally a baby is born, glistening with liquid. Already his cells are cooperating. His muscles limber up in jerky, awkward movements; his face recoils from the harsh lights and dry air of the new environment; his lungs and vocal cords join in a first air-gulping yell.
>
> Within that clay colored, wrinkled package of cells lies the miracle of the ecstasy of community. His life will include the joy of seeing his mother's approval at his first clumsy words, the discovery of his own unique talents and gifts, the fulfillment of sharing with other humans. His is many cells, but he is one organism. All of his hundred trillion cells know that they will some day be united into the person God created them to be.

Let there be no mistake. Conception is ordained and orchestrated by God and life begins at conception. Some cultures add nine months from birth to the age of a person in realization that life does begin at conception, and birth is just another milestone in the life cycle.

No one can legitimately and honestly look at the facts of fetal development and not draw the conclusion that once a sperm and egg unite, a person is created and all persons under our law are entitled to life, liberty and the pursuit of happiness.

CHAPTER EIGHT

THE ISSUE IS LIFE

"Thou shalt not kill." Exodus 20:13

Now that we have determined that life is sacred and divinely conceived, the logical conclusion in the abortion debate is that the issue is human life, nothing more, nothing else and nothing less.

Here is where people get twisted up in the debate. They either ignore the Biblical and biological facts, or they try to argue their position based on something other than the issue of life.

I was a debater in college, and in my political career I have engaged in many debates. One thing I learned early on about winning a debate is the importance of pulling the other side off the main issue and then debating instead on some lesser issue.

Those who support abortion want to argue on social, economic, child abuse and a whole host of other bases. To win the issue, we must stay focused on life.

The facts are simple. A sperm and ovum unite to form what some would call a product of conception. But that product of conception becomes its own individual person, totally separate from the mother other than, of course, the fact that the mother has the sacred custodianship and ability to protect and nurture during the period of gestation.

As we have seen in the previous chapter, within days of conception, the baby is circulating blood, often not even the same blood type of the mother. When conception takes place, another distinct person becomes a reality.

Most people know that fetuses are human beings. To what other species would they belong? Still, there are those who claim that babies aren't human until after birth, and that being human doesn't give you the right to live. These kinds of absurd statements have helped to stir up both the abortion and personhood debates and mostly results in more people to turning in the direction of pro-life. But more of that in the final chapter.

Another thing I have learned in debating is that a good debater needs to know all of the facts on all sides of the issue. In fact, in some actual debates, teams don't know which side they will argue until the flip of a coin at the beginning of the debate.

Therefore, I have tried to study and understand all aspects of the abortion debate. However, I must say that the facts are so one-sided that it would not be an acceptable college debate subject.

Modern technology has gone a long way to aid understanding of fetal development. I marveled thirty years ago when we first saw a sonogram of our third child. It was new "state of the art" technology, yet it still looked like a black moving blob with occasional views of appendages.

Then, more recently, we saw the four-dimensional image of one of our grandsons. It was as if we could reach out and hold him! All of his features were so clear. How could anyone deny he was a person? You can see him for yourself, as his face is on the front cover of this book.

THE ARGUMENTS FOR THE PRO-LIFE POSITION ARE SO COMPELLING. ONE NEED ONLY LOOK AT THE FACTS.

The arguments for the pro-life position are so compelling. One need only look at the facts. Sadly, many don't, as we will see in the next chapter.

Once we have proven that life begins at conception, the logical conclusion is that the intentional taking of that life is fetal homicide or murder. It is an act in direct contradiction of the commonly accepted idea of the sanctity of human life. Civilized societies prohibit people from intentionally taking the life of another person. Abortion is not different than one adult taking the life of another person without cause.

Adoption is a viable alternative to abortion. It accomplishes the same result without taking the life of the baby. The birth mother disposes of the baby, but rather than extinguishing the baby's life, the baby goes to a loving home and lives a normal life.

In my early years of practicing law, I kept a list of couples who wanted a baby but were unable have a biological child for various reasons. When I would get a call that an out-of-wedlock young woman was pregnant, I would try to match a soon to be born infant with a couple longing to be parents. Pastors that knew I wanted to match unwanted infants with parents would often call when situations arose in their congregations.

When the day of birth came and the baby was ready to be discharged, my secretary would pick up the infant. We would present the baby to its new parents in my library. It was always a glorious experience!

Not long ago, I was having coffee in a café when a fire truck pulled up and the crew came in for coffee. One large fireman walked over to my table and asked if I was Senator Grant. I said, yes, and he replied by telling me who he was and reminding me that thirty years prior I had "given" him to his parents. He just wanted to say thanks.

I remember the case well. His parents had tried unsuccessfully for ten years to have a baby. They were eventually both found to be medically incapable of having children. Finally they came to me asking if I could help with an adoption, and, obviously, I was able to do that. Quite interestingly and not an uncommon story, within six months the couple got pregnant.

Another case I remember is a doctor and his wife who could not have children. They had adopted two girls, but also wanted a boy. Later, a man came to my office to tell me that the woman he was dating had a teenage daughter who was pregnant but they didn't want to abort. He asked if I could help place the child. I asked if they knew the sex of the child, and he said, "Yes, it is a boy." I told him I could solve his problem, and I did.

I still occasionally see the child I placed. He is a teenager and a fine looking young man. Thankfully, even though he came along after Roe, his biological parents wanted to preserve his life for the enjoyment of another couple, and thank God that they did.

I believe there is no such thing as an unwanted child. People are standing in line waiting for a baby. But I have heard people whisper behind the backs of someone with a special needs child that they bet they are sorry they had that child.

Tell that to my doctor friend who has a Downs Syndrome child they love so much. Or mention that to another friend of mine who has a mentally retarded child. The child loves Jesus and tells everyone about Him with childlike faith.

Tell that to the parents of Tim Tebow, one of the greatest collegiate athletes to ever play the game. Tell that to thousands of Florida Gator fans who still bask in the glory of two national championships because of a baby whose doctor had advised his parents to abort him.

Justin Bieber has made waves around the world for proclaiming himself pro-life. But a new interview his mom gave to the Today Show's Kathie Lee Gifford provides an extraordinary background as to why Bieber may oppose abortion - his mom chose life.

Justin Bieber's mother, Pattie Mallette, explained to the viewing audience in that interview about the sexual abuse she suffered before becoming pregnant. She was determined to make it through a difficult pregnancy situation and give birth to Bieber. Drugs and alcohol abuse had caused her to be deeply depressed.

At the age of 17, Mallette became pregnant with Justin, and at the time, she was encouraged to abort the baby. Mallette said that was an option she couldn't consider. She said, "I just knew I couldn't. I just knew I couldn't. I just knew I had to keep him,'" she told Gifford, "and, do the best I could. I didn't know how I was going to do it. But I just knew that I couldn't abort. I had to do my best. I had to see what I could do. And I was determined to do whatever it took." (Life News.com, September 17, 2012)

Mallette went on to say that the first time she heard her son cry, it was literally music to her ears. "I know this sounds crazy, but he sounded like he was singing". "He did, she said, "It was like this, like, "A hah, a hah." And I was like, "Oh my gosh, it is so precious and amazing. I just want to squeeze him."

In the February 2011 interview that made headlines, Rolling Stone magazine initially reported Bieber said, "I really don't believe in abortion. It's like killing a baby."

Justin Bieber is entertaining millions in audiences all over the country, not just because he is a good singer and entertainer, but because his mother chose life rather than death for her son.

Unfortunately, after Roe, I found very few opportunities to place a child. Today in America there are thousands of couples who want to adopt a baby. In this country, there is no such thing as an unwanted baby. There is a wanting home for every available baby.

Many people have to go to Russia, China and African countries to adopt children. Our nieces and nephews and their families recently adopted international children and we know of many other families who have rescued children from all parts of the globe.

Abortion not only takes the life of the child being aborted but can also be a barrier to later creation of life. Even under the most excellent of conditions and procedures, there is a risk in future ability to bear children. Many women have had an abortion and now wonder why they cannot get pregnant. Earlier, I mentioned my aunt as a close and real example.

Many abortions, even from licensed facilities, do not provide the proper protections for pre-op and post-op complications. Often this "procedure" is done in doctor's offices or clinics which are ill equipped to handle hemorrhaging or other life-threatening consequences.

Abortion is inherently unsafe to the mother. Physical problems from abortion can include hemorrhage, infection, sterility and even death. Women also often experience "severe" or "intense" pain during an abortion.

Psychological effects can include depression and mental trauma often leading to divorce and suicide.

The psychological effects of an abortion are so well documented that psychologists have grouped them under one name: post-abortion syndrome (PAS). Women may experience symptoms of PAS right after the abortion, but oftentimes PAS does not manifest itself until many months or years after the abortion.

Symptoms of PAS are recurrent memories, dreams of the abortion experience, avoidance of emotional attachment, relationship problems, sleep disturbance, guilt, memory impairment, hostile outbursts, and substance abuse.

Fathers, grandparents, and siblings can also experience the psychological effects of abortion.

In the instance of rape and incest, I am most sympathetic. When I was a prosecutor, I prosecuted rape cases and my interviews with victims were often very emotional, especially when the perpetrator was a member of the family.

Sympathy has caused many pro-life people to call for legalized abortion in cases of rape and incest, but two things have to be remembered.

The issue is life. God breathed life, and regardless of the circumstances of conception, it is wrong to take a human life. Abortion punishes the unborn child who committed no crime.

Abortion should not be used as another form of contraception, nor should it be confused with contraception. Physical contraceptives(condoms, IUD's, diaphragms, etc.) or chemical contraceptives(birth control pills) prohibit or impede the uniting of sperm and egg. This should never be compared to the tragedy of taking the life of an unborn child after it is conceived.

For women who insist on complete control of their body, there are many ways to prevent pregnancy (and unwanted sexually transmitted diseases) by the responsible use of contraception while still engaging in recreational, out-of- wedlock sex for those who choose to do so.

As a taxpayer, I am opposed to my tax dollars going to fund abortions through numerous government sources. To me that is morally wrong.

The marketing secret of the abortion industry is to move fast. Often the mothers are in shock and are traumatized upon having discovered they are pregnant. Fifty-two percent of women obtaining abortions in the U.S. are younger than 25. Women aged 20-24 obtain 32% of all abortions. Teenagers obtain 20% of all abortions and girls under 15 account for 1.2% according to The Center for Bio-Ethical Reform.

Young, frightened girls who are often minors, and many operating without their parents' knowledge or consent, have insufficient life experience to fully understand what they are doing. Abortion clinics want them to agree to an abortion as soon as possible lest they have a change of mind. Many have life-long post abortion regrets.

There are many reasons why abortion is the wrong "choice," but it still goes back to the issue is life. Abortion is the murder of an unborn human being. If you have a stomach for it and want irrefutable proof that abortion is the taking of a human life, go to the Internet and see a procedure for yourself.

The evidence demands the verdict that abortion is fetal homicide. How long will we allow it to continue in our land?

CHAPTER NINE

THE ENEMY IS AN INDUSTRY

"Be sober, be vigilant; because your adversary the devil, as a roaring lion, walketh about, seeking whom he may devour."
1 Peter 5:8 KJV

Prior to Roe vs. Wade, there were no licensed abortion clinics in the United States because the procedure was totally or partially illegal in all fifty states. However, post Roe, an industry quickly sprang up.

Today, it is believed that there are nearly two thousand clinics across the land. . However, since so many abortions are performed in physician's offices, these statistics are misleading. But by any measure the number is huge and the procedure is very profitable. In fact, abortions are so profitable that many clinics are run by chains or franchises.

Consider these facts:

- Over 1.29 million babies were killed by abortion in the United States in 2002. (The Guttmacher Institute: http://www.guttmacher.org/media/presskits/2005/06/28/abortionoverview.html November 1st, 2007.)

- Over 48 million babies have been killed by abortion in the United States since the Roe vs. Wade decision. (National Right to Life Abortion Statistics: http://www.nrlc.org/abortion/facts/abortionstats.html November 1st, 2007.)

- Approximately 42 million abortions occur each year worldwide. (Health Day: http://www.healthday.com/Article.asp?AID=609085 November 1st, 2007.)

- Abortion killed 73 times more Americans than died in battle in our last 12 wars combined. (America's Wars: U.S. Casualties and Veterans: http://www.infoplease.com/ipa/A0004615.html November 1st, 2007.)

- To equal the average number of abortion deaths in one year, the terrorist attack on the World Trade Center would have had to have been more than 400 times more lethal.
- Abortion worldwide kills more people every 2 months than the Holocaust did in 12 years.
- The 54 million American people who have been killed by abortion equal approximately 16 percent of the current population of the United States.
- The number of people killed by abortions since 1973 exceeds the current populations of each of the 50 states, including California.
- Almost 1 out of every 4 American babies is aborted. This number is greater than the current populations of Sweden, Norway, Lithuania, Latvia, Ireland, Iceland, Finland, Estonia, and Denmark COMBINED.
- It would have taken about 342 Hiroshima-type nuclear attacks to kill as many people as abortion has killed since Roe vs. Wade.

Many former employees have "come out" of the abortion industry and reported how it really works. It is not about women's health. It really is not about abortion. It is about making money.

Consider the story of Carol Everett, whose descent into the abortion industry began after she aborted her third child in 1973, under pressure from her husband and doctor. After the abortion, her life began to fall apart. She subsequently had an affair, started to drink heavily and eventually left her husband.

With a psychiatrist's help, she got her life together enough to go to work for a medical supply company. That job eventually led her into the abortion industry. Working for an abortionist showed her how much money could be made in the abortion business, so she decided to open her own clinics.

She told her story to the first "Meet the Abortion Providers" conference in November 1987:

We opened our clinic and the first month we did 45 abortions. The last month I was there, with two clinics functioning in the Dallas area, we did over 500 abortions a month in that clinic. I was compensated at the rate of $25.00 per case plus one-third of the clinic's revenue, so you can imagine what my motivation was. I sold abortions.

I had made $150,000; was on target in 1983 to make $260,000; and when we opened our five clinics, I would have been taking home about a million dollars a year. I expected to make more than that after we were functioning.

At the time, we were planning to open the five clinics there were some problems between the partners. We decided to call in a business counselor and worked with him for thirty days. It turns out this man was a preacher. He told me that God had sent him because there was someone in there that the Lord wanted out. I left in 27 days.

I'm sure you've seen those numbers advertised that say "Problem Pregnancy," "Abortion Information," or "Pregnant?" When a young girl finds out she is pregnant, she may not want an abortion. She may just want information.

But when she calls that number that's paid for by abortion money, what kind of information do you think she is going to get? Remember, they sell abortions. They don't sell keeping the baby. They don't sell giving the baby up. They don't sell delivering the baby in any form. They only sell abortions.

The counselor that the girl speaks to on the telephone is paid to be her friend. She is supposed to seduce her into a friendship of sorts to sell her the abortion.

I cannot tell you one thing that happens in an abortion clinic that is not a lie.

There are usually two questions the girls ask. The first is: Does it hurt? "Oh, no! Your uterus is a muscle. It's a cramp to open it: a cramp to close it; it's a slight cramping sensation. Everybody's had cramps - every woman in the world."

Then they ask: Is it a baby? "No, it's product of conception; it's a blood clot; it's a piece of tissue."

When the girl goes in for the abortion she pays up front then goes into a room for counseling. They give her a 6 to 12 page form. This form is written by an abortion attorney to confuse the girl to death. It works and she doesn't ask any questions. She goes back to the two questions: Does it hurt? Is it a baby?

I cannot tell you one thing that happens in an abortion clinic that is not a lie.

I CANNOT TELL YOU ONE THING THAT HAPPENS IN AN ABORTION CLINIC THAT IS NOT A LIE.

I've never been able to come up with the words to describe the abortion procedure. There are no words to describe how bad it really is. It kills the baby.

I've seen sonograms with the baby pulling away from the instruments that are introduced into the vagina. And I've seen D & C through 32 weeks done without the mother being put to sleep. Yes, they are very painful to the baby. But, yes they are very, very painful to the woman. I've seen six people hold a woman on the table while they did the abortion.

After the abortion, the girls are brought to the recovery room where there are two reactions. The first reac-

tion is: *"I've killed my baby."* It amazed me that it was the first time they called it a baby and the first time they called it murder. That is probably the healthiest reaction. That woman is probably going to have the ability to walk out of there and deal with it, and perhaps be healed and move on.

The second reaction is: *"I am hungry. You have kept me in here for four hours, and you told me I'd only be here for two. Let me out of here."*

She is running from her abortion. She is not dealing with it; she's choosing to deny it. They say it's now an average of five years before people actually deal with the fact that, yes, they did kill their baby.

The girls that walk out of there are the lucky ones. We were seeing over 500 abortions per month and doing one a day second and third trimester abortions. We didn't use the laminaria, we did all the dilation on that one day and we were seeing a tremendous amount of complications.

Yes, we had a death. A 32-year old woman with a 17-year-old son and a 2-year-old son. Never made the papers. Her boyfriend felt guilty for his part in the abortion, and he didn't want to deal with it. Her family thought, yes, she had probably had an abortion, but they didn't want to deal with it. It never came out. No lawsuit.

Then there was the girl who the doctors decided had a fibroid tumor at the back of her uterus. That's a highly common tumor that's very rarely malignant. The two doctors decided they were just going to pull it out after her abortion. They didn't know they were pulling on the back of her uterus, and they pulled the uterus out wrong-side-out of a 21-year-old; she had a hysterectomy.

Let there be no mistake, the abortion industry is big business putting profits first and women's health second.

From 2005 to 2006, Planned Parenthood, the nation's largest abortion provider, increased the number of abortions it performed from 264,943 to 289,650. With that increase, total revenue was over 1 billion dollars. The profit margin (excess revenue over expenses) went from 55.7 million to 112 million. This included taxpayer dollars in the form of government grants and contracts in excess of $336 million dollars (Planned Parenthood Federation of America, Annual Report 2006).

Planned Parenthood lobbies our government to remove abortion restrictions in order to continue to assure future financial profits. In 2006, Planned Parenthood Political Action Committees spent 53.1 million dollars to adjust public policy. (Planned Parenthood Federation of America, Annual Report, 2006)

More adoptions mean decreased profits: there is no financial motivation for Planned Parenthood, or any abortion provider to offer adoption referrals. In 2006, Planned Parenthood increased the number of abortions performed by 48%. In that same year, adoption referrals decreased by 81% (Planned Parenthood Federation of America, Annual Report 2006).

Abortion providers have high doctor turnover. Included in the upcoming RHA legislation in New York State (Reproductive Health Act) is an agenda item to demote the licensing requirements for professionals who perform abortions. Instead of requiring abortions to be performed by medical physicians, the requirement has been lowered to allow "qualified licensed health practitioners" to perform abortions. This broad terminology can be interpreted to allow nurse practitioners or other health care workers to perform abortions. The ramifications of this change in medical requirements are detrimental to the health and safety of women.

The motivation behind this change is to ensure the abortion industry a steady supply of professionals willing to perform abortions. Licensed physicians are increasingly hesitant to perform abortions and leave their positions much sooner than do physicians who practice in other areas of medicine.

The number of U.S. abortion providers is on the decline. Between 2000 and 2005, providers decreased by 2%. By 2005, 87% of all US counties lacked an abortion provider. (Jones RK et al., Abortion in the United States: incidence and access to services, 2005, Perspectives on Sexual and Reproductive Health, 2008, 40(1):6? 16.)

Abortion clinics give their employees training in successful sales tactics. Smiling models in Yellow Page ads and on the internet appeal to women in distress by promising safe, comfortable and confidential abortion services. Clinics are designed to have a "spa like" atmosphere and nurses and clinicians are trained to play into to a woman's fear, uncertainty and sense of urgency in order to close the abortion deal. (Light of Life, Mission City)

The slick sell techniques effectively eliminate or greatly restrict informed choice. Vulnerable and frightened young girls are victims of targeted marketing and slick sales pitches. Long before they know what they are doing, it is done.

Time is not always a luxury we have, but when we do, it almost always works in our favor. The longer the time between an initial visit to an abortionist and when they return for the actual procedure, the greater the chance the mother will decide against it.

That is why I, along with many others, fought so hard to slow the process down and in the process to educate the mother. We tried legislating a waiting period. After all, we have a three-day waiting period for purchasing a firearm, just in case someone in a heat of anger would buy one to kill another person. Why not a waiting period before killing a baby?

We tried requiring a sonogram which would give the mother the opportunity to view the image. We have also tried other educational means to help the mother make an informed decision.

The proposal that made the most sense and was consistent with existing law would have required parental notification and consent before the procedure could be performed on a minor. That is the legal requirement for all other medical procedures.

I remember when our daughter injured her ankle while in high school. The school was unable to contact us for a number of hours while our minor daughter was in pain. They could not even take an x-ray without our permission.

But not so with an abortion. It is a procedure with serious potential medical consequences. The courts have ruled that it is a matter of privacy. Young girls can get pregnant, get an abortion, and the parents never know.

Needless to say, the giant pro-abortion lobby was successful in striking down most of these types of legislation. The ones that got through met their fate before the bar of the courts.

It is important to understand that we are not fighting just a woman's choice. We are fighting a well-funded industry which stands to lose billions if abortion is restricted or eradicated.

In the years since the US Supreme Court ruled to legalize abortion up to the ninth month of pregnancy, the battle over the right to life has become a deeply entrenched and polarizing issue in American political life.

A new study suggests that feminist ideology is no longer the driving force to keep abortion legal, but rather more sinister motives of commerce and profit are keeping the billion dollar abortion industry alive and growing.

Catholic San Francisco, the newspaper for the Archdiocese of San Francisco, reported that Vicki Evans, the Respect Life Coordinator for the Archdiocese of San Francisco's Office of Public Policy and Social Concerns, authored a study finding that market forces are now deeply intertwined with the abortion industry that supplies them with "fetal parts, tissues and cells." Pharmaceutical and cosmetic companies often use aborted fetal material in their products.

Evans' study, "Commercial Markets Created by Abortion: Profiting From the Fetal Distribution Chain", was written as the thesis for her license in bioethics from the Regina Apostolorum Pontifical University in Rome.

In this study, Evans looked to discover how certain "special interests" or a "commercial cause" rather than the graying adherents of feminist ideology that first clamored for legal abortion was at work to keep abortion legal and the transactions in aborted fetal material largely unmolested by regulators in a virtually clandestine market.

"It is important to shine a light on these practices that take place behind closed doors," wrote Evans. "There are powerful forces conspiring to keep this information from the public and the media with the ostensible conviction that they are protecting a woman's right to choose.

"However, it is becoming obvious that many ideological groups are being used as pawns by powerful financial interests."

It could not have been said any better. The enemy is an industry!

CHAPTER TEN

THE HOLOCAUST

"O LORD, how long shall I cry, and Thou wilt not hear! even cry out unto Thee of violence, and Thou wilt not save!"
Habakkuk 1:2

When someone mentions the word Holocaust, we are conditioned to immediately think of the mass slaughter of Jews by the Germans during World War II. But Holocaust is defined as "any mass slaughter or reckless destruction of life."

Under that definition, certainly, there have been many holocausts and ethnic cleansings throughout history. Along with the German Holocaust, abortions have to be at the top of the list because none other has taken as many lives.

Are abortions fundamentally different from the German Holocaust? To answer this question, let's compare the Nazi Holocaust to abortions, including the gruesome partial birth and born alive types, in America today.

- The Germans killed a million Jews every year over a six year period. America's abortionists kill more than that each year and have been doing it since 1973.
- The Germans disposed of unwanted Jews who they considered to be not fully human. The abortionists dispose of unwanted babies who are also legally considered to be not fully human.
- Both sold body parts. For the Germans it was usually gold dental work. For the abortionists of today it is stem cells and the like.
- Both disposed of bodies as trash, and many of them were killed by licensed physicians.

Some day, those with blood on their hands will be asked why they didn't try to stop it.

The guilt we cast upon the Nazi-era Germans today for not stopping the Jewish holocaust will one day be cast upon us by future generations for the holocaust of our babies, and rightfully so.

THE GUILT WE CAST UPON THE NAZI-ERA GERMANS TODAY FOR NOT STOPPING THE JEWISH HOLOCAUST WILL ONE DAY BE CAST UPON US BY FUTURE GENERATIONS FOR THE HOLOCAUST OF OUR BABIES, AND, RIGHTFULLY SO.

How did it happen? Andy Andrew's book *How Do You Kill 11 Million People?* (Thomas Nelson) sheds a lot of light on this issue.

His answer is quite simple and still used by some elected leaders to achieve various goals today. How do you think someone could kill 11 million people?

YOU LIE TO THEM

Reading the testimony at the Nuremberg Trials, the rounding up and transporting of people to the death camps (there were some 1,500 of these camps) presented a challenge, and the solution was to have them go peacefully.

This was done by telling the Jews that they needed to congregate to specific locations where they would be in fenced-in enclosures for their own protection from those who would want to harm them.

Then they were told they were being transported to safe havens where life would be enjoyable and safe. With these assurances, they walked peacefully to the railroad depots. It wasn't until after a hundred people were shoved into a cattle car designed to hold eight cows and the door locked that they realized their fate.

They had been the victims of an intricate web of lies, delivered in stages and designed to ensure the cooperation of the condemned (but unknowing) Jews.

Adolf Eichmann directed the operation with precision. According to sworn statements, these were very likely his exact words:

> *Jews: At last it can be reported to you that the Russians are advancing on our eastern front. I apologize for the hasty way we brought you into our protection. Unfortunately there was little time to explain. You have nothing to worry about. We want only the best for you. You will leave here shortly and be sent to very fine places indeed. You will work there, your wives will stay at home. Your children will go to school. You will have wonderful lives. We will all be terribly crowded on the trains, but the journey is short. Men, please keep your families together and board the rail cars in an orderly manner. Quickly now, my friends, we must hurry.*
>
> (Neal Bascomb, Hunting Eichmann
>
> (New York: Houghton Mifflin Harcourt, 2009, 6)

Dietrich Bonhoeffer was one of the great Christian apologists in the early twentieth century, writing a number of books on theology and Christian apologetics.

Bonhoeffer sought to halt the genocidal slaughter of the Jews and others. It is impossible to read the works of Bonhoeffer and not see a stark parallel to the abortion holocaust of today.

In his last book, *Ethics*, written shortly before he was hanged, he stated: "Destruction of the embryo in the mother's womb is in violation of the right to live which God has bestowed on this nascent life."

Matt Barber (WND Commentary, July 6, 2012) writes, and I concur:

> *So it occurs to me that those who call themselves "pro-life" and put faith to action in defense of innocent*

persons, as did Dietrich Bonhoeffer, honor both the memory of this Christian martyr and the God he served. They have picked up his mantle. They are continuing his noble work.

By contrast, if pro-lifers are modern-day Dietrich Bonhoeffers, then what does that make abortion supporters? In the years leading up to and during World War II, many Germans, who were otherwise generally good people, succumbed to Nazi propaganda and acquiesced to the horrific Jewish persecution that escalated from a slow boil to a red-hot torrent around them. In effect, they bought into exactly the same kind of dehumanizing, euphemistic semantical garbage embraced by those who today call themselves "pro-choice."

Mind-boggling is the human capacity to rationalize genocide.

Perhaps one of the best works on Bonhoffer and the abortion parallel has been written by Eric Metaxas. ("Bonhoffer"), Thomas Nelson, April 2010).

On Feb. 2, 2012, Metaxas gave the keynote address at the annual National Prayer Breakfast in Washington, D.C. He was clearly inspired and influenced by the subject of his latest biography.

Sharing the stage and sitting merely feet away was President Barack Obama, the most radically pro-abortion president in U.S. history. In a spectacular show of resolve and moxie, Metaxas walked over to the president and handed him a copy of "Bonhoeffer."

While President Obama squirmed nervously in his seat, Metaxas addressed both his book and the abortion holocaust with incisive clarity, saying, in part, "We are capable of the same horrible things. Apart from God we cannot see that they (the unborn) are persons as well. So those of us who know the unborn to be human beings are commanded by God to love those who do not yet see that. We need to know that apart from God we would be on the other side of that divide, fighting for what we believe is right. We cannot demonize our enemies. Today, if you believe abortion is wrong, you must treat those on the other side with the love of Jesus."

Barber continues and sums it up well:

Indeed, we are admonished in Scripture to pray for our enemies, to love those who do evil.

Nonetheless, we are also commanded to speak truth. We are told to hate that which is evil and to fight, indeed to die if necessary, for that which is good.

Indeed, ours is a holocaust no less real, no less evil than that perpetrated by the Nazi regime. We've simply moved from the gas chambers to the abortion clinic, from Auschwitz to Planned Parenthood.

I love America. She's the greatest nation on earth. Nonetheless, as long as we continue to allow this enduring slaughter of the most innocent among us, we are no better than was Nazi Germany. Abortion on demand will be viewed by our progeny as the single greatest blight on our American heritage.

To live under Roe v. Wade is to live in shame. To live under pro-abortion leadership is to live under the Fourth Reich.

The abortion industry has used some of the same tactics. How do you get more than fifty million mothers to murder their own babies?

YOU LIE TO THEM

Like the Jews were led to slaughter, young mothers are being lied to and led to abortion clinics by commission-based sales persons. Mothers are told that nearly all abortions take place in the first trimester, when a fetus cannot exist independent of the mother. As it is attached by the placenta and umbilical cord, its health is dependent on her health, and cannot be regarded as a separate entity as it cannot exist outside her womb.

That is either a half-truth or a total lie, solidly proven by examination of genetic structure. The baby's health is dependent on the mother's health until it is born. If people were to buy this lie, then how can they support subsequent trimester abortions and partial birth abortions when the baby is partially outside the womb?

The concept of personhood is different from the concept of human life. This is another lie, human life and personhood cannot be separated and occur simultaneously.

To further illustrate this devaluing of life, an article in the March 29,2013 issue of *The Weekly Standard* shed light on the true position of Planned Parenthood:

> *Florida legislators considering a bill to require abortionists to provide medical care to an infant who survives an abortion were shocked during a committee hearing this week when a Planned Parenthood official endorsed a right to post-birth abortion.*
>
> *Alisa LaPolt Snow, the lobbyist representing the Florida Alliance of Planned Parenthood Affiliates, testified that her organization believes the decision to kill an infant who survives a failed abortion should be left up to the woman seeking an abortion and her abortion doctor.*

Another lie is that adoption is not an alternative to abortion. It remains the woman's choice whether or not to give her child up for adoption. That may be true, but they also say that a woman has a choice whether or not to murder her baby. One is good for the child and the other is execution of the child. That is hardly a logical comparison.

Incidentally, statistics show that very few women who give birth choose to give up their babies - less than 3% of white unmarried women and less than 2% of African American unmarried women. Once they see the miracle of birth and realize that it is a product of their body, they seldom want to give it away.

Mothers are lied to about the safety of an abortion. They are being told that an abortion is a safe medical procedure. Even if an abortion is done in a safe environment, the procedure does turn out all right for a vast majority of women. But they are not told or they are lied to with regard to possible serious complications including a woman's long term mental and physical health and the statistics of their ability to become pregnant or give birth after an abortion.

Those getting pregnant in the case of rape or incest are told that the psychological harm of carrying the baby to term is worse that the mental anguish of having an abortion. Studies have proven just the opposite to be true.

As theologian and ethicist Dr. Michael Bauman has observed:

> "*A child does not lose its right to life simply because its father or its mother was a sexual criminal or a deviant. Furthermore, the anguish and psychic suffering caused by rape and incest has been treated quite effectively.*" (Michael Bauman, "Verbal Plunder: Combating the Feminist Encroachment on the Language of Religion and Morality," paper presented at the 42nd annual meeting of the Evangelical Theological Society, New Orleans Baptist Theological Seminary, New Orleans, Louisiana, Nov. 15-17, 1990, p. 16.)

Professor Stephen Krason points out in the following statement that:

> "*Psychological studies have shown that, when given the proper support, most pregnant rape victims progressively change their attitudes about their unborn child from something repulsive to someone who is innocent and uniquely worthwhile.*" (Stephen M. Krason, Abortion: Politics, Morality, and the Constitution Lanham, MD: University Press of America, 1984), p.

284. For an overview of the research, see Sandra Kathleen Mahkorn, "Pregnancy and Sexual Assault," in David Mall and Walter F. Watts, M.D., The Psychological Aspects of Abortion Washington, D.C.: University Publications of America, 1979, pp. 67-68.)

Another lie mothers are told is that abortion is not used as a form of contraception. The opposite is the case. Now, I must admit that no woman in her right mind would want to go through an abortion, and I am sure that few plan it that way. But the point is that greater sexual freedom and more carelessness is encouraged by the fact that if all else fails, abortion is always a viable alternative.

The big sales pitch is the ability of a woman to have control of her body being critical to civil rights. Take away her reproductive choice and you step onto a slippery slope. On this I agree, at least to the "her body" part.

A woman should have the choice of whether or not she wants to have sex and to what extent she wants to protect herself from pregnancy. That is her choice.

A woman should have the choice of whether or not to get a tattoo anywhere on her body or to have a wart or other growth removed from her body. If a woman wants no more children, then sterilization should be a choice for her body.

But the operative in the choice argument is "her body." Once a woman becomes impregnated, there are two bodies....... two distinct bodies, one within the other.

The mother has the sacred custodianship for nine months to nurture and care for the unborn child she is bearing.

How can a woman have a partial birth abortion after nine months and call it abortion, but if she delivers the child and throws it in a garbage can, it is called murder and is punishable as such? There is no logic.

The mother may be able to speak for her body, but who speaks for the baby, the most innocent and unprotected of all?

With all of this in mind, let's revisit the raw statistics:

- *Annually, 42 million babies die from abortion worldwide. That's approximately one baby being aborted every two seconds.*
- *An estimated 54 million American babies have been aborted since Roe was decided in 1973. Approximately one out of every four pregnancies in America is terminated by abortion.*
- *Slightly over half of all women having abortions are in their twenties and eight out of ten report a religious affiliation (43% Protestant, 27% Catholic and 8% other religions).*
- *41% of aborting women are white, 32% black and 20% Hispanic.*
- *98% of abortions are a matter of personal choice with only 1.7% for health of the mother and .3% resulting from rape or incest.*

No wonder it is comparable to the Holocaust. Murder is murder whether it is of the innocent in the womb or someone in the neighborhood.

CHAPTER ELEVEN

CHOICE: WHO SPEAKS FOR THE BABY?

"This day I call heaven and earth as witnesses against you that I have set before you life and death, blessings and curses. Now choose life, so that you and your children may live."
Deuteronomy 30:19

Choice! That seems to be the battle cry of the pro-choice movement. They talk about a woman's reproductive freedom and her right to choose what she does with her body.

But my question is, who speaks for the baby? After all, he or she is a separate person temporarily housed in the mother's womb. Pro-choice for who?

Are they talking about the right to choose the ultimate method of contraception or the baby's right to choose to continue its life?

May we never forget that abortion is the ultimate form of child abuse, both for the aborted baby and for those underage girls who go through the procedure.

Whose right to choose are they talking about, the mother's or the baby's? After all, there are two distinct people involved and the choice of one is fatal to the life of the other.

Let's look for a moment at how our society protects children. Those under the age of adulthood lack the right to make many legal and binding decisions, including the decision to undergo medical procedures without consent of a parent or legal guardian.

Look what happens when a child is mistreated. Authorities will remove the child and place it with a court appointed guardian or in a foster home. All of this is for the protection of the child who lacks the legal and physical capacity to make decisions on its own.

If a mother mistreats a child, no matter how young, she can be criminally charged and can permanently lose the custody of her child.

As a lawyer, I wrote many wills, and usually the number one question of younger clients was how they could guarantee who would get the custody of their children in the event of the demise of both the mother and the father.

Often and usually, much to their surprise, I would advise them that their children, unlike other tangible and intangible items, were not their property and they could not bequeath them like other property.

I would tell them that they could make suggestions for the court to follow as to post-death custody. But ultimately, the court would rule in favor of what was best for the child.

I would also tell them that if they think they "own" their children, just mistreat them and see how fast they are taken away.

Now, if our society goes to such lengths to protect children from birth to the age of adulthood, then why are mothers, in the name of choice, allowed to terminate their baby's life?

The answer is simple. The courts, despite overwhelming evidence to the contrary, simply deny personhood to the unborn and therefore deny the protection of the law. To be consistent with post-birth protections, doesn't it make sense that before an abortion, the court should be required to appoint a guardian ad litem to speak for the best interests of the baby?

Admittedly that is a stretch of the imagination, but it makes perfect logical and legal sense. The only way to get around it is to declare that the unborn baby is legally denied personhood under the law. And in order to do that, one would need to deny all Biblical and biological evidence to the contrary.

Actually, "choice" is an improper word to use for those "choosing" to have an abortion. If you look up the definition of choice it is: "Choice consists of the mental process of judging the merits of multiple options and selecting one or more of them."

In other words, choice is a cognitive process of weighing the merits of various alternatives and selecting one or more of them. This is exactly why the abortion industry operates on a "Do it now without time to think" process. They don't want women to be informed about alternatives or have time to weigh the consequences of different decisions.

The abortion industry's goal is to get them into their clinic and do the procedure before they have time to evaluate their decision to abort. Once the abortion is over, there is no turning back. No wonder the industry opposes every proposed idea that would slow down the process or help women understand alternatives.

Once the deed is done, it is done, but the pain and damage lingers. Read the following typical anonymous story published on www.standupgirl.com.

> *My story is long. I could tell you all the facts, the "supposed" reasons why it was logical to go through with the abortion. My age and circumstance in the end will not matter. I can say my fear and confusion and pressure from others was the same felt as most of us before we decided to have the abortion.*
>
> *What I will say is that I cannot go a day (really no more than a couple hours) without feeling the pain in my heart, the ache and the longing for someone that was in my life and now is gone. It will not go away. Random tears at the sight of a mother and child will happen.*
>
> *That is a certainty. Anger and self-hate will be yours on frequent occasion too. Oh and don't forget that every month remembering that first time you found out that you were pregnant and that secret joy that you weren't supposed to have will be mixed with memories of cramping and the blood that you saw after your baby was violently taken from your body.*
>
> *Oh did I remember to tell you that if you are fortunate to have children present or future that you will never be*

able to look in their eyes without wondering what your unborn child's eyes would have looked like, their smell, what their skin would have felt like. Your arms will always feel empty.

I know God forgives and He still loves me. I don't think I am an awful person unworthy of love. I get along in my life, go to work, love many, and laugh often. But if you asked me who I am? I would have to say I am a sad, sad woman who would give anything to change the decision I made on that July 9th. I want my baby back, I want to feel my baby back in my belly, grow inside me and kick me. I want to see that child of mine grab their toes as babies do, smile that gum-less baby smile, fall asleep in my arms, grow to be a beautiful child, grow to be a wonderful being in this world. I want my baby back.

Stories like this are shared or kept secretly tucked away in the minds of millions of women, like Amy, who have aborted.

When I was in our state legislature, I was always looking for ways to impede or find alternatives for abortion. One day I received a call from Governor Jeb Bush who asked me to file a bill, which we dubbed "the firehouse bill." I agreed to do so, and I am happy to say that it passed and now is law.

The idea resonated with me, because I had recently been talking with someone at the city sewer treatment plant who told me how often baby parts would be found in the sewer filters. He explained that some women carry to term, and then deliver and flush. It was a horrible thought. I felt there must be another alternative, and the firehouse bill was it.

The law provided that a woman may drop off a newborn baby (three days young or less) at a local firehouse where paramedics would receive it with no questions asked. This protects the life and health of the baby and protects the anonymity of the mother.

It also protects the mother from otherwise existing laws on child abandonment.

Strange arguments arose against the bill. For instance, a legislator who had vehemently fought against granting paternal rights to enable parents to influence and guide daughters in the abortion decision now opposed the firehouse law on the basis that the baby's father would never know.

Others said that for the good of the baby's future health, there ought to be medical history from both of the parents. Well, certainly that would be helpful, but it would also defeat the whole purpose of the law. When the choice is a dumpster or a firehouse, I will take the firehouse any time.

The reasons for opposition defied logic, but the answer of why they rose up is simple. It would reduce the number of abortions and eat into the industry's lucrative cash flow. As a matter of fact, through 2008, nearly a hundred babies were saved through this law and many more babies have been saved because of it since then.

Many states have passed "firehouse" laws and many are considering other protective legislation. In Ohio, for example, the House passed H.B. 125 which would prohibit the abortion procedure on any baby that had a fetal heartbeat that can be detected, generally six to seven weeks into pregnancy. Unfortunately, it did not pass the Senate.

In the course of committee hearings, Melissa Ohden testified. She was the victim of a botched abortion. She testified about how the abortion affected her.

She was burned alive in her mother's womb by a saline poison injection in August of 1977, when her mother, an unwed college student who was five months pregnant, made a "choice." That "choice" burned Melissa's lungs, organs and skin. She was left for dead and thrown in the trash with the medical waste. When a nurse heard her and saw her moving, Melissa was taken to a hospital and treated.

Here is part of her testimony:

There was some commentary in the media after last week's hearing before this committee that somehow, preborn children would oppose legislation such as Bill 125, aptly named the Heartbeat Bill. I am here today as a woman who, as an infant, survived a failed abortion attempt, to emphatically deny such a claim, to lend a voice to my fellow 53 million preborn brothers and sisters who have lost their lives since Roe v. Wade, and our fellow Americans yet to be born, who are at risk of being aborted.

As a survivor, I believe that I can speak for all of the children like me who have been aborted or those who are at risk of being aborted, in saying that we support this bill, and we urge you to do the same. It may somehow be easy for some to deny the right to life of a child in the womb when you never hear their heartbeat, when you never come face to face with them as a fellow human being, but what if you did come face to face with them? Who in this room wants to look me in the eye today and tell me that I was not worth protecting from abortion? Who in this room wants to tell my daughter that her mother's life, and therefore, her life, was not worth defending? What is the pro-abortion lobby going to say: "I'm sorry our "choice" didn't work and you made it out alive??

Are they really so heartless as to say Melissa belonged in the trash with the medical waste? You can read more of Melissa's story at http://www.melissaohden.com.

Only the most hard-hearted can see a baby with a beating heart and refuse him or her protection.

Choice? For who, mother or baby? The logic is inescapable.

The truth is out. Those who call themselves "pro-choice" can still pretend we're living in the dark ages, but the witnesses, the technology and the facts speak otherwise.

CHAPTER TWELVE

TOLERANCE

"I charge you in the presence of God and of Christ Jesus, who is to judge the living and the dead, and by his appearing and his kingdom: preach the word; be ready in season and out of season; reprove, rebuke, and exhort, with complete patience and teaching."
2 Timothy 4:1-2

Tolerance has become the battle cry of the left in a lot of areas, not the least of which is abortion. In its more pure sense, tolerance means a fair, objective, and permissive attitude toward opinions and practices that differ from one's own.

In that sense, tolerance has long been the fabric of American culture. Under our freedom of speech, we are free to express our opinions without fear of reprisal and with mutual respect that people may well have differing positions on any given subject.

However, quite unfortunately, showing respect for those having differing positions has become rather one-sided. I should be respectful of other's opinions, but if I am against same sex marriages, then I am a bigot or homophobic.

Unfortunately, we live in a time of moral relativism, a theory built around the claim that there is no true morality. Many young people want to set their own rules, but your right to swing your fist ends at the end of my nose.

It is impossible to set rules and laws without a platform of cultural morality, and without rules and laws, there is anarchy.

During the twenty-one years I was in public office, I voted about twenty-five thousand times, and many of those votes had moral consequences.

People say that morality cannot be legislated. Well, the last time I checked, most of the Ten Commandments have been written into law, and surely they fall into the definition of morality.

Those who oppose legislation outlawing abortion (fetal homicide) claim that since it is based on Biblical principles, to enact it would be to legislate morality. Well, what do they say about laws prohibiting murder (adult homicide)? Is that not the legislation of morality?

Francis Beckwith well-stated the abortion morality issue in his work, *Arguments from Tolerance,* as follows:

> Some abortion-rights advocates argue that it is simply wrong for anyone to "force" his or her own view of what is morally right on someone else. Consequently, they argue that pro-lifers, by attempting to forbid women from having abortions, are trying to force their morality on others.
>
> It does not seem obvious that it is always wrong to impose one's morality on others. For instance, laws against drunk driving, murder, smoking crack, robbery, and child molestation are all intended to impose a particular moral perspective on the free moral agency of others. Such laws are instituted because the acts they are intended to prevent often obstruct the free agency of other persons; for example, a person killed by a drunk driver is prevented from exercising his free agency. These laws seek to maintain a just and orderly society by limiting some free moral agency (e.g., choices that result in drunk driving, murder, etc.) so that in the long run free moral agency is increased for a greater number (e.g., less people will be killed by drunk drivers and murderers, and hence there will be a greater number who will be able to act as free moral agents).
>
> Therefore, a law forbidding abortion would unjustly impose one's morality upon another only if the act of abortion does not limit the free agency of another. That

is to say, if the unborn entity is fully human, forbidding abortions would be perfectly just, since abortion, by killing the unborn human, limits the free agency of another. Once again, unless the pro-choice advocate assumes that the unborn are not fully human, his or her argument is not successful.

(The Abortion Debate: Arguments from Tolerance by Francis Beckwith, Article ID:

DA020-2, Christian Research Institute)

So we circle back to what I have said in practically every chapter of this book and will say again: the abortion debate rises or falls on the issue of when life begins. If you are drawn off of the issue of life and onto others, you lose. But if you stay on point and hammer on the issue is life, you win. It's that simple.

I have asked many pro-abortion women to closely examine the biological facts, including the fact that abortions can legally be performed after a time when the baby could survive outside the womb. If they can honestly and intellectually examine those facts and draw the conclusion that it is not a human life, then I respect their right to support abortion. So far, I have had no takers.

Unfortunately, some claiming to be pro-life have exercised violence, even murder, against abortion clinics. This behavior is wrong and it is sad, but a few extremists don't represent the pro-life movement.

However, when such acts of violence happened, the pro-abortion biased media flew the flag as if these acts were an official part of the pro-life movement.

Likewise, similar acts of hatred and violence have been exercised on the other side as well.

How well I know, because I have had numerous death threats against my family and me. For some time we were under constant protective guard. Picket lines were assembled around our home to prevent entrance and exit. Our property was subjected to physical destruction. My office was destroyed and a bomb detonated in front of our home.

Thankfully, none of us were injured, but the interesting thing is that the press chose neither to air nor to print the first word about these acts against me. Large portions of the media establishment have abandoned any pretense of objective journalism on these kinds of issues.

Once, a local radio station said that if my legislation passed, abortions would return to the back alleys and be performed with coat hangers. When they encouraged their liberal listening audience to deliver coat hangers to my office, I got enough to start a dry cleaning business.

I once objected to a leading homosexual being paid $25,000 of state money to celebrate gay pride on one of our university campuses. My objection started a well-orchestrated national media campaign saying I was against free speech. I said it's quite the contrary. I was all for freedom of speech, and I thought that if he came on campus, he ought to give a speech, but he should not receive state taxpayer funds for doing so.

What we have created in society and in the press is a sort of "moral illiteracy." We need leadership to bring us back to an awareness of the moral fabric of America.

During the 2012 Iowa Presidential debate, former Senator Rick Santorum was asked if he would approve an abortion exception for rape and incest. Here is his answer:

> *"The Supreme Court of the United States on a recent case said that a man who committed rape could not be killed, could not be subject to the death penalty, yet the child conceived as a result of that rape could be. That to me sounds like a country that doesn't have its morals correct. That child did nothing wrong. That child is an innocent victim. To be victimized twice would be a horrible thing.*

It is an innocent human life. It is genetically human from the moment of conception, and it is a human life, and we in America should be big enough to try to surround ourselves and help women in those terrible situations who have been traumatized already. To put them through another trauma of abortion; I think it's too much to ask and so I would absolutely stand and say that one violence is enough."

What the tolerance issue really boils down to is a belief by some that one side should tolerate the views of the other side without attendant reciprocity.

A few months later, speaking at the 2012 Republican National Convention, Santorum added:

"I thank God that America still has one party that reaches out their hands in love to lift up all of God's children -- born and unborn, and says that each of us has dignity and all of us have the right to live the American Dream." The line, met with deafening applause and one of the longest standing ovations of the night, was the culmination of Santorum's emotional telling of his daughter Bella's struggle with a rare genetic disorder that doctors predicted would leave her with a life not worth living.
"The doctors later told us Bella was incompatible with life and to prepare to let go," Santorum said. "They said, even if she did survive, her disabilities would be so severe that Bella would not have a life worth living."
"We didn't let go and today Bella is full of life and she has made our lives and countless others much more worth living," he added, his eyes welling with tears.

Welcome to the world Roe has created. A world where children simply do not matter. A world where the only thing that matters in the end is what adults want.

I saw and experienced first-hand the tolerance (or lack thereof) when I filed the Defense of Marriage Act. Who would have ever thought that such legislation would be necessary? But as same sex unions began to take hold, the need arose.

We have already talked about creation, but I know that if you want a chicken, you need a hen and a rooster. God created Adam and Eve, not Adam and Steve.

GOD CREATED ADAM AND EVE, NOT ADAM AND STEVE.

I was not then and neither am I now suggesting that government ought to control how people of any sex relate to each other in their private social and physical relationships. Though I believe it is wrong for me to engage in such conduct, I respect the right of people to do as they please behind closed doors. They will ultimately give that account to God, not to me or to the government.

However, to grant marital or some other legal status to same sex couples flies in the face of creation and common sense. It was a bill that had to be filed, so I did.

It was called the Defense of Marriage Act, which specifically stated that marriage is the "union between one man and one woman" and barred the state from recognizing same-sex marriages performed in other states.

The following is a news and press release summary of the proceedings:

The 1997 Florida Legislature responded to the same-sex issue by overwhelmingly enacting the Florida Defense of Marriage Act. In response to Governor Chiles' decision to let the bill become law, the bill's senate sponsor, John Grant, stated he thought it was "Great that the Act takes effect on June 4, right smack dab in the middle of Gay Pride Week."

The major thrust of the Act, in accordance with the Federal Act, is to prevent same-sex couples from lawfully marrying in Hawaii and subsequently migrating to Florida to claim the rights, privileges, and immunities granted to different-sex couples in Florida. The Act also expressly codified the present Florida ban on legal recognition of same-sex marriages.

The Act was a major part of the new Republican majority's 1997 legislative agenda. Florida House Speaker Daniel Webster went on record in late January, pledging his support for the legislation. Senator Grant began spurring the debate as early as December 1996, stating that "God created Adam and Eve, not Adam and Steve, and it was never intended that there be a lawful contract of marriage between same-sex people."

Several committees considered the bill, including the Senate Judiciary Committee. Senator Grant introduced the bill, stating that "Florida law provides that a marriage relationship is one man and one woman. Generally, organized civilization for about 6000 years has defined that as the definition of marriage." (FOR BETTER OR FOR WORSE: A CRITICAL ANALYSIS OF FLORIDA'S DEFENSE OF MARRIAGE ACT MICHAEL J. KANOTZ[*] Copyright (c) 1998 Florida State University Law Review)

I was amazed when I went to many of my colleagues to ask them to co-sponsor the bill that many expressed support and said they would vote for it if it got to the floor. But these colleagues added that they didn't want to offend their "gay" constituents with an election looming.

We will talk later about our "hide behind the tree" supporters, but suffice it to say that many of those supporters surprised me by doing what they could to keep it off the floor calendar.

On these defining issues of our time, we need leadership who will stand up and speak or get out of the way.

In the end, it came to a vote and passed 37-3, and when signed by the governor, it became the first of its kind in the nation.

Meanwhile, I returned home to find the windows of my office smashed and shattered and the words "gay power" spray painted on the wall.

So much for tolerance.

CHAPTER THIRTEEN

CRISIS PREGNANCY CENTERS: THE FIRST LINE OF DEFENSE

No discussion of abortion would be complete without a discussion of the role played by crisis pregnancy centers across America. They are our greatest source of strength in the ongoing fight against abortion.

According to the Guttmacher Institute, there were 1.21 million abortions performed in the United States in 2008, the most recent year for which data is available. This amounts to 3,322 abortions per day. (Jones, Rachel K. and Kathryn Kooistra. "Abortion Incidence and Access to Services in the United States, 2008." Perspectives on Sexual and Reproductive Health 43, no. 1 (2011, March): 41-50)

Since many abortions are done in women's health centers that perform other services and some are done in hospitals, it is difficult to determine the number of facilities performing abortions, but the numbers are generally estimated to be less than a thousand.

Planned Parenthood is the largest abortion provider in America. Seventy-eight percent of their clinics are in minority communities. African-Americans make up 12% of the population, but account for 35% of the abortions performed in America. For every two African American women that get pregnant one will choose to abort. An African-American baby is 5 times more likely to be killed in the womb than a white baby. (Guttmacher Institute)

Recently, the board of Planned Parenthood of South Central New York voted unanimously to change its name and sever ties with the national organization, Planned Parenthood Federation of America. The reason: Abortion.

Abortion is critical to Planned Parenthood's bottom line. In 2010, they mandated that all Planned Parenthood affiliates must perform abortions starting in 2013. The South Central New York affiliate isn't taking a pro-life position. It simply saw no reason to duplicate procedures offered by other doctors and clinics in the area. But its decision is a reminder that Planned Parenthood isn't really about "women's health." (Gary Bauer, Campaign for Working Families 12/03/12)

Suffice it to say that no one has any difficulty finding an abortion clinic ready to meet their needs and to do it promptly.

A crisis pregnancy center (CPC), sometimes called a pregnancy resource center (PRC), is a non-profit organization established to counsel pregnant women against having an abortion. CPC's generally provide peer counseling related to abortion, pregnancy, and childbirth, and may also offer additional non-medical services such as financial assistance, child-rearing resources, and adoption referrals. CPC's that qualify as medical clinics may also provide pregnancy testing, sonograms, and other services.

There are over 4,000 CPC's in the United States, and their outreach has been very effective. By giving caring and informative information to women about their babies, thousands of lives have been saved. (Jones RK, Kooistra K (March 2011). "Abortion Incidence and Access to Services In the United States, 2008". Perspectives on Sexual and Reproductive Health 43 (1): 41,50. doi:10.1363/4304111. PMID 21388504)

CPC's are such a threat to the abortion industry that a counter attack has been launched on the Internet and elsewhere to discredit them.

The following is from one site sponsored by Planned Parenthood: http://www.plannedparenthood.org/health-topics/pregnancy/standard-21507.htm:

> Deciding what to do about an unplanned pregnancy can be very difficult. It may be made even more difficult by so-called "crisis pregnancy centers." These are fake clinics run by people who are anti-abortion. They have a history of giving women wrong, biased information to scare them into not having abortions.

Here are some factors that CPC's have to deal with each day to counter what the opposition is doing.

Planned Parenthood's Record Year

According to Gary Bauer, writing from the Campaign for Working Familes, 2011 was a good year for the abortionists at Planned Parenthood and a bad year for American taxpayers and innocent babies in the womb. According to various reports, Planned Parenthood performed a record number of abortions -- nearly 334,000 in 2011.

It also reported assets in excess of $1.2 billion, received a record $542 million in taxpayer funding -- 45% of its annual revenue -- and had more than $87 million in "excess revenue." That would be profits for a supposedly non-profit organization concerned about "women's health."

There is absolutely no moral justification for American taxpayers to be subsidizing the nation's largest abortion provider. But there is no economic justification either.

Bauer cites the following facts:

Facts About Teen Pregnancy (Courtesy of dosomething.org):

The U.S. has the highest teen pregnancy rate in the industrialized world, twice as high as in England or Canada.

- 2006 saw the first rise in the U.S. teen pregnancy rate in 15 years. An estimated 750,000 teens will become pregnant this year.
- About 1 in 3 women become pregnant at least once before they're 20.
- A sexually active teen who does not use contraceptives has a 90% chance of becoming pregnant within a year. Teen pregnancy affects education --- only a third of teen mothers earn their high school diploma. And only 1.5% have a college degree by age 30.
- Teen pregnancy also affects their kids. Girls born to teen mothers are more likely to be teen mothers

themselves. Boys born to teen moms are more likely to end up in prison.

- 75% of girls and over half of boys report that girls who have sex do so because their boyfriends want them to.
- 8 in 10 girls and 6 in 10 boys say they wish they had waited until they were older to have sex.
- Most teens (6 in 10) and adults (3 in 4) believe that teen boys often receive the message that they are "expected to have sex."
- Sexual activity increases the risk and incident of teen depression. Depression leading to suicide is the 3rd leading case of death among teens. (Courtesy of STDepidemic. com)

It is obvious that the CPC's are making inroads. With slim budgets and few paid employees, the CPC's depend heavily on volunteers who share my passion for protecting the lives of the unborn.

The cover of a recent *World Magazine* (June 26, 2013) shows babies that were saved through the efforts of CPC's.

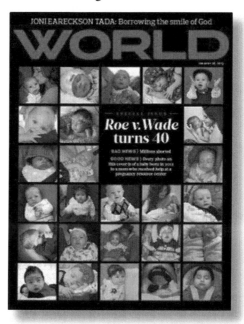

The bottom line is that CPC's are the abortion industry's greatest nightmare, as they multiply while abortion clinics are closing.

A number of years ago, my wife volunteered to be on the board of one of our local CPC's and over the years, we have watched it grow. First there was a mobile unit and now most recently the opening of a new facility right next door to an abortion clinic!

Noted author, pastor and speaker Dr. Bruce Wilkinson, has led the founding of The Great Turnaround, which is an effort to reach out and assist local CPC's in raising one hundred million dollars to save one hundred thousand lives. Already it is having an incredible impact with CPC's across America.

There is a direct relationship between the size of the budget of a CPC and the number of babies saved. It is a simple formula. Raise more money = save more babies.

CPC's provide shelter in a storm. These pregnancy centers will not only help a mother to give birth, but they will also find her assistance if she wants to keep her baby, or help the mother find a good home for her child through adoption. Sure, they'll never have the big donors or flashy celebrity support that the abortion centers have, but they are making a real difference in the lives of these women and their babies, pre-born and born.

The CPC's have been under attack by the abortion industry, and we have had to defeat a lot of laws against them. For example, in New York, where 41% of all pregnancies end in abortion, Then Arch Bishop and now Cardinal Timothy Dolan released a formal statement concerning Intro 371, the bill before the New York City Council that would require crisis pregnancy centers to, among other things, display signs detailing the services that they do not provide, like abortion. Dolan stated:

> *"This controversy over Intro 371 reminds me of a conversation I had not too long ago with a dedicated woman medical professional who works in one of the wonderful crisis pregnancy centers here in New York City. "Archbishop," she said to me, "we're here to help*

women who want an alternative to abortion. We don't get massive subsidies from the government like the abortion clinics. We sure don't have the well-heeled donors Planned Parenthood has. Why are some people trying so hard to get rid of us? Why is the city government harassing us? All we want is to be left alone to do our work."

Why is the abortion industry attacking the CPC's? The answer is simple, CPC's have effective ministries. They tell women the truth. They provide them with alternatives. They help them understand the nature of the baby they are carrying. And they shower them with love and share the Gospel with them in most cases.

One of my pro-life all time heroes is Pat Layton. While busy with life and running an insurance agency, God called her to open the first CPC in our city. Over the years, Life Impact Network/A Woman's Place has saved countless lives under Pat's guidance and leadership.

Not only has she saved countless babies through her *Surrender the Secret* groups and a book of the same name, she has helped many women who have resorted to abortion in the past to recover from the emotional wounds and trauma that all too often follow an abortion.

With her permission, I want to share with you the story of Pat Layton:

"Surreal is the best word to describe my feelings as I walked down the long, white hospital corridor leading into the Neonatal Intensive Care Unit of Tampa's largest Woman's hospital. White walls, white ceilings, and bare windows. An emotional battle raged in my heart and head. My husband and I walked the seemingly endless hallway together, just as we had so many years before.

This day we were here to meet our soon-to-be baby daughter. Our hearts were drawn to meet her. My head was stuck in memories of another time when we had taken a similar walk, down a different corridor, in this same hospital. Twelve years before, we'd had an abortion there. It all seemed so bizarre. The circumstances of each event were amazing unto itself.

As Mike and I rounded the corner of the NICU into the open nursery area, we were both trembling, gripping hands so tightly as to cut off all feeling. The room was filled with babies. Most were inside of clear plastic boxes with two little "portholes" in the front for the doctors and nurses to slip their hands through when caring for the sick and tiny babies. Some babies lay naked with tiny arms and legs flailing wildly and all kinds of tubes and wires attached to them for monitoring of every body function. They lay on chest high podium-like tables covered with soft, white sheepskin.

That is how we first saw her. A tiny baby girl. TINY being the key word. The nurses had named her Julianna. Juli for the July month of her birth, and Anna for the prophetic beauty of the name. Julianna had been born to a 16 year old girl at approximately 23 weeks gestation. Her birth weight was a whopping 1-1/2 pounds! She was 10" long. The day we met Julianna, she had recently undergone some surgery and had dropped to only one pound. She was barely the size of a matchbox!

She was without question, the most incredible and beautiful thing I had ever seen. As I looked upon her face for the first time, doctors and nurses had gathered around to see for themselves the couple who had come upon the scene to adopt Julianna. They were very protective and concerned. I was in a trance. It took all that I had to contain my balance and not swoon to the floor as I heard the sweet voice of God speak to my heart,

"This, Pat, is what I create in a mother's womb, this is why I have called you to do the work I have called you to do." I felt overwhelming surety that God had literally placed a "pre-born" child in my presence.

As I looked upon Julianna, my mind was reeling from that very reality, "the work" He had "called me to do." I was very certain that God had called me not many months before to open Tampa, Florida's first Crisis Pregnancy Center. As I stood beside that tiny baby lying in the center of that white, sheepskin table, a large group of my closest friends were hard at work back at my insurance agency, painting, wallpapering, and preparing some vacant space in the back half of my office to become a Crisis Pregnancy Center. I had "recruited" them to join up with the vision God had given me and they had eagerly responded. We were set to open in just a few more months.

God was clearly leading the way. His favor preceded our every move. I was running my own insurance business out of the front office and preparing for ministry out of the back. Donations were coming from every direction; paint, wallpaper, office supplies, pregnancy tests, furniture, on and on the blessings flowed.

From the moment I had asked Christ into my heart, June 4, 1984, He moved into my life in a mighty way. He surrounded me with strong, Christian mentors who were committed to helping me learn as much as I could about God and His ways. They taught me to love the Word of God and to pray. They were relentless in their unconditional love as the many walls of my past and my pain had to be crumbled in my life as I was set on a whole new path. The Lord knew how important these friends would be to me as I struggled to believe that He could truly forgive a past as sinful as mine had been.

I will never forget the day that He gently revealed the truth about abortion to me. My immediate temptation was to hide away and never tell my Christian friends. I was convinced that once they knew the horrible truth, they could not accept me anymore. Of course, I was very wrong. Not only did they accept and love me, they became the wind under my wings as they encouraged me into the plans God had for my life. What an awesome God He is, thinking through every detail!

As I stood amidst the flurry of activity within the NICU, my thoughts swirled over the events of the past few days...

My life was in a non-stop wave of activity as I daily ran a full-time insurance agency, parented two sons: an 18 year old senior in High school, and a pre-teen 10 year old. All the while, I was deeply involved in the excitement of preparing the way for the Crisis Pregnancy Center.

It was deep in this time when my husband, Mike, woke up one morning and announced, "I think we should adopt a baby girl!" My response wasn't exactly overflowing with Proverbs 31 when I responded in my old Pat-ways with, "Are you crazy! Can't you see how busy my life is? Does it look like I have time for a baby? Besides, we have a senior!" Needless to say, I was shocked and a bit miffed.

We had discussed the possibility of adoption on several occasions. We had two sons and I had longed for a daughter for many years. I had always believed in my heart that my aborted child was a little girl. It has just never happened. Too expensive. Too much red tape. Where do you start? Time passed and it was only small talk. Until that day I told Mike it was impossible. Bad timing. No way! Fortunately with God, NOTHING is impossible. His ways are not our ways!

Mike arrived home from work that same afternoon looking frazzled and pale. He had taken the liberty, as only a man would do, of inquiring of an attorney friend of ours that day at work about the possibilities of adopting a child, maybe a toddler. "Do you believe in divine intervention?" the friend asked Mike. "Absolutely... why?" Mike asked his friend.

Our friend proceeded to tell Mike that he had just hung up the phone with the hospital and they had a little baby girl whose birth mother desired to place for adoption. Our friend knew that the sixty-something families he had on his list would probably be skeptical about this adoption. He proceeded to tell Mike, "this little girl was born three months early and she weighs only one pound. She is likely to have serious life-long health challenges. She will possibly be blind, unable to hear, and could be retarded. It is difficult to determine and probably will be for a long time. We are not even certain she will live." Mike relayed our morning conversation to our friend, promptly assuring him that I would probably not be interested, but he would talk to me that night.

We sat on our bedside as my husband relayed the remarkable story to me that evening. We were both overwhelmed with emotion. In typical "Pat" fashion, I got right to work. I decided to call everyone I knew who was interested in adopting a child. The first one I called was one of my very dear "God friends," Elaine.

Elaine and I had become friends through a ministry we had founded together called, Sisters of Rachel, a healing ministry for women who have had abortions in their past. Elaine had an abortion in her late teens. That aborted child turned out to be the only child she would ever conceive. She was unable to become pregnant again and longed for a child. She was the first one I called.

She listened intently to Julianna's story. Then she was very quiet on the other end of the telephone. "What do you think, Elaine?" I asked her. "I think I would absolutely love to have that little girl, but I can't," she replied.

"Why not, Elaine? God will work this out. He can bring this child through, I know He can" I told her. "Oh, I am certain that He will bring her through, Pat, but this baby is not for me…God planned this little girl for you and Mike!"

I can remember the chair I was sitting in, the level of the sun outside the window, the clarity of the blue sky, and the tears that rolled down my cheeks. She IS for me. That little tiny girl that I have never seen is going to be my daughter. Mine and Mike's. Julianna IS for us. I called Mike at work and we agreed to meet at the hospital to see our daughter for the first time.

It was love at first sight for both of us. We knew immediately and without a single moment's doubt that God had delivered Julianna to us. Mike and I spent the next three months going back and forth to the hospital. Sometimes twice in a day. Each time I went to see Julianna, I would lay my hands upon her in her isolate and pray Psalm 139 and Jeremiah 1 over her. "Julianna, God knit you together in your mother's womb, you are fearfully and wonderfully made. God knows the plans He has for you, Julianna. They are plans for good and not for evil, you will live and not die."

Mike and I and all of our friends and family stood in faith for complete and perfect health for our baby girl.

It was not an effortless or faultless faith. Sometimes, I would cry all the way home from the hospital and ask Mike, "what if she dies?" He would gently remind me of how God had pulled this together and that even if she did, God had planned for us to be her Mommy and Daddy. She needed us.

Sometimes our friends and family would weaken, not so sure about just what we were getting into. We became very close to Julianna's doctors and her main nurse, Jayne. As we did, we learned more and more of the miracle details of her birth and her rescue from death. Not a single NICU team member could deny the miracle of her life or of her undefeatable spirit. Mike and I were always aware of what an honor and a privilege we had been given.

Julianna came home with us on October 23, 1988. She was three months old. She had a head full of blonde hair, perfectly-shaped tiny, rosy lips and beautiful pink skin. She was a perfectly healthy four pounds. No complications. No health problems. Nothing missing, nothing broken.

Soon after we brought Julianna home from the hospital, a wonderful older lady, who was a friend and volunteer for the CPC, came forward and announced to me that God had instructed her to make herself available to help me with Julianna so that the CPC could open as planned. "Grandma Wooley" stood by my side and helped me with Julianna whenever I needed her until she went into the first grade. She is still very much a part of our lives and Julianna adores her.

On many occasions I would take Julianna into the CPC with me, and when a young girl would come to the center with abortion on her heart, I would bring Juli-

anna into the counseling room, place her in the young girl's arms, and say, "precious friend, this is what God knits together in a mother's womb." Many children are alive today as a result of one of those moments."

Today, Julianna is twenty-four years old. She loves God and she loves life! She is now studying for her exam to be a Nurse in the NICU at Woman's Hospital, the very same hospital where she was rescued as a 1 1/2 pound baby so many years ago! Is that neat or what?

Pat's story has been repeated over and over again as people have been inspired to open crisis pregnancy centers. They are without a doubt our first line of defense in the war against abortion.

CHAPTER FOURTEEN

WHAT CAN YOU DO?

"Look and be amazed at what's happening among the nations!
Even if you were told, you would never believe what's taking place
now."   *Habakkuk 1:5*

What can you do? The answer is, a myriad of opportunities, and each of us must get involved and be active. We cannot be spectators, but must be participants if we are going to win this battle. As we will see in the final chapter, the tide is turning, but there is a long way to go.

Are you one of those who say you are pro-life when you get a telephone survey or one who says you think abortion is wrong in a casual conversation around a bridge game? Or are you seriously interested in getting involved?

We will win, but it will take a lot more than idle talk and depending on others. I encourage you to volunteer. As Christians, we are called to involvement and action.

The Christians of the Roman Empire had no political power. If called on to act against God's laws, they could simply say no and endure the consequences. But in free governments like ours, we have the right and duty to participate and make changes.

As Christians, we are called on to be active in our world, bringing God's transforming love into every part of our lives….. home, school, work and politics. God works through his Church to bring the transformation that began with the resurrection.

I am afraid that on the abortion issue we curse the darkness but fail to light candles of hope and help.

Where is the Church? In his recent book, *Futurecast,* (Carol Stream, IL: BarnaBooks/Tyndale House Publishers) George Barna analyzed the state of Christianity in America today. His findings said much about the failure of the Christian community to rally to the cause.

Eighty-five percent of Americans identify themselves as Christians and eighty-four percent consider the Bible to be a holy or sacred book. The typical American owns four of them.

Let's try to put that into perspective. While more than four of every five Americans identify themselves as Christians and consider the Bible to be a holy book, this land has experienced moral and spiritual decay like never before.

It seems that there is a short circuit between what people say they believe and how they act and live. This also applies to Biblical/social issues like abortion.

Sexual sin is rampant and pornography on the Internet is big business, as are strip clubs and other sexually oriented establishments. Business is brisk.

The Bible calls Christians to be different from the world. Paul tells us not to be conformed to the world but to be transformed. He tells us to not be overcome by evil, but to overcome evil with good. (Romans 12:12)

How is it possible for the Church to be salt and light to a lost world when its members appear to be no different than the rest of the world? "Do not be afraid; keep on speaking, do not be silent." Acts 18:9b

As you are forming your world view and searching Scripture for God's truth on all kinds of matters, it is important to understand God's stance on the controversial parts of a Christian world view today.

Abortion is one of the issues you need the most courage to speak up about. People within and without the Church will argue with you passionately on the issue of abortion. It takes courage to stand up against strong, worldly, peer pressure.

The pro-life movement is hated by so much of the world, but sadly, many Christians would rather clam up than stand up, because they either don't want confrontation or they are ill equipped to debate the issue.

The Church needs to be equipping its people to defend a Christian world view, and that is one of the reasons I chose to write this book. If I claim to be a Christian, then I must believe that every life is sacred.

As a case in point, a friend of mine passed along this scenario to me:

> *I had a networking lunch with a gentleman and he started the conversation about politics. His words: "I hope as a woman you're not voting for the pro-life candidate." My response was, "Well, I happen to be one of those women who believe that life begins at conception and the right to life needs to be protected." His response was, "Well you can't make abortion illegal." My response was, "If it is illegal to give birth and dump your baby in a garbage can, why shouldn't it be illegal to kill your baby a week earlier, or a month earlier or 9 months earlier?" He went on to say, "You and I aren't going to agree on this." That was the first thing the two of us agreed on. Surprisingly, when our lunches arrived, he asked, "Do you mind if we pray?"*

Some Christians simply don't comprehend that life is the issue. In Luke 6:46, Jesus asks the provoking question: "Why do you call Me, 'Lord, Lord' and not do what I say?"

On the issue of abortion, the "Church" in general is not doing what Jesus said. Another recent Barna poll (www.barna.org 4/18/12) revealed that only 29% of all likely voters placed abortion high on their list of issues that could affect their vote in the next election.

Among evangelical voters, abortion ranked third as the most influential issue behind health care and taxes, at 58%. We are not doing a good job educating people in the world, but worse, we are not doing a good job of educating people in the Church.

Only six in ten Americans believe that abortion ends a human life and only half believe that abortion is morally wrong, yet it remains a terrible stain on our nation.

Many Christians seem to have bought into or been sold on a secular world view. They need to be taught to stand up against the world's opinion.

Jesus said, "Whoever acknowledges me before others, I will also acknowledge before my Father in heaven." Matthew 10:32

Rick Warren recently said: "To live with uncommon courage and stand up for Christ, you have to learn how to clarify your world view - what you base your beliefs on. You also have to understand the non-Christian world views that compete for your devotion every day." (Daily Hope, September 14, 2012)

Part of the problem is that the abortion industry has done a better job of "selling" its pro-abortion propaganda than churches have done promoting the Gospel.

Many churches stay away from social and political issues, because they don't want to offend anyone or lose contributions and membership. Some churches have been so brainwashed that they believe that speaking out on social and political issues could cause them to lose their tax status.

Perhaps our greatest enemy is the "silent supporter," those who claim to be pro-life and do nothing about it. In an earlier chapter I spoke of the book, *How Do You Kill 11 Million People*, and I noted how people were lulled into compliance by being lied to.

Well, there is another side of that sad story and it is the people who turned their backs and did nothing. It is said that when the trains of screaming captives passed by a church on Sunday mornings, they simply turned up the music so they wouldn't hear the screams.

That is happening today as people – church people – turn their backs on the facts and do nothing to help solve the problem. Did you ever consider that if you spent one day a month volunteering in a crisis pregnancy center, you might save just one life, and that would make your ministry service such a very worthwhile experience?

Abortion is not necessarily a political issue. It is a social, moral and Biblical issue. Though they may be debated in a political context, the real issues facing America today are not scientific, economic and technological. They are moral and theological, and the Church must speak out to forge public opinion.

Though the polls show the national opinion on abortion to be split about evenly, the passion and the involvement on the pro-abortion side is far greater than those of us on the pro-life side.

The role of the Church is to challenge, educate and to create passion for the sanctity of life and then muster a mighty army of Christian soldiers to go to the front lines of abortion and make a difference.

> **THE ROLE OF THE CHURCH IS TO CHALLENGE, EDUCATE AND TO CREATE PASSION FOR THE SANCTITY OF LIFE AND THEN MUSTER A MIGHTY ARMY OF CHRISTIAN SOLDIERS TO GO TO THE FRONT LINES OF ABORTION AND MAKE A DIFFERENCE.**

Sadly, many Christians are ill-equipped and not educated to understand and be involved in the political process. I remember when I first got elected, someone in the Sunday School class I was teaching suggested that I would have to resign as teacher because of the separation of church and state!

Unfortunately, the percentage of those registered to vote and those who actually vote is not much different within the church than in the community at large.

When I was in office, I used to keep a computer print-out of the precincts within my district. When someone called, I would quickly check to see if they were registered and had voted in any of the past four elections. It's a matter of public record.

Once a group of five people were trying to start an "anti-Grant" campaign in their neighborhood because of a bill I had filed regarding a homeowner's assessment fee, which I was asked to file by the civic association.

I asked my aide to call each one and invite them to the office. To my surprise they all showed up. As I sat down around the conference table, one admonished me not to get too comfortable as they were going to take the seat away from me in the next election.

I told them it was their right if they chose to, but they needed to get started. My comment surprised them when I said that I knew how they could get five guaranteed votes against me the following day. I told them they should register to vote since none of them around the table were registered voters.

The best time to get an office-holder's vote on an issue is before a candidate gets your vote in the election. We must identify people of true moral character and courage and become involved in the political process to get them elected. Likewise, we need to defeat those who support abortion and do not understand that the issue is life.

I well remember back in my early days right after Roe, no one suspected that we would ever have to vote on any abortion issues. The Supreme Court had settled it.

Candidates would tell people whatever was expedient on the "life" issue but would not have to deliver. When the Governor called a special session on abortion, there was a collective gasp. It didn't bother me. I had told people what I believed and how I would vote and I was prepared to do it.

Later, as abortion legislation began to flow, members would file a bill to satisfy some constituent and then make sure it was never placed on the agenda for a committee vote. Briefly, I was a candidate to be president of the Senate, but I soon dropped the idea when many whom who I had hoped would support me said they were opposed to my candidacy. They said they knew I would make them vote on all that "family and moral stuff."

Political cowards who claim to be on our side will hijack the calendar. You can ask a person if they are pro-choice or pro-life, but the real question, like in a Texas poker game, is: "Are you all in?"

Political correctness has run amuck. We are afraid to say or do things that might offend someone, and some subjects are just not proper to talk about.

Dr. Ben Carson is an internationally renowned neurosurgeon and humanitarian. His story is the story of the American dream, overcoming incredible odds to become what he has become.

Yet when Carson was invited to give the commencement address at Emory University recently, there was great opposition once students and faculty members learned that Carson had faith in Christ and disdain for evolution. (World Magazine June 2, 2012 p. 11).

There is a double standard and it goes back to "tolerance" discussed earlier. If, instead of Dr. Carson, some anti-Christian liberal had been invited, it would have been hailed as an exercise in academic freedom.

The abortion issue has divided us right down the middle like no issue since slavery.

My purpose in writing this book is to nail down that the issue is life, not to advocate any particular candidate or party or office. My purpose is to give backbone to the litmus test for holding public office, in either party, for it is the judges and legislators and the political parties in power who will ultimately make the decisions on which way the abortion debate will fall.

Your job is to become educated on the issues and facts and to seek out candidates who don't just give lip service on the life issue or take the position following the polls. Your job is to identify the candidates who are "all in," and then do everything you can to get them elected and keep them in office.

A good indicator is also the platform of a political party, written each fours years just prior to a presidential election.

The 2012 Democratic Party made abortion rights a major theme at their convention. They didn't just promote legalized abortion. They defended partial birth abortions in which babies in their sixth and seventh month of pregnancy are brutally aborted by puncturing their skulls.

They refused to condemn sex selection and "coin toss", (deciding which twin to keep) abortions, and they insisted that taxpayers pay for abortions. They opposed any parental involvement when it comes to abortions for minor children. (2012 National Democratic Platform)

It is also interesting that the party that promotes "diversity" officially rejected an effort by pro-life Democrats to get the party to include them in its platform that calls for keeping unlimited abortions legal and paid for at taxpayer expense.

Kristen Day, executive director of Democrats For Life of America, says the platform panel refused to acknowledge any difference of opinion on abortion within the Democratic Party. (DNC Rejects Bid to Include Pro-Life Democrats in Abortion Plank by Steven Ertelt Washington, DC LifeNews. com 8/16/12)

The Democratic Party also added a plank favoring same-sex marriage after it was advocated by the President.

Quite the contrary, the Republicans once again have a strongly pro-life platform. They reaffirmed the call for a human life amendment and legislation extending 14th Amendment protections to unborn children by passing yet another solidly pro-life platform on the issue of abortion which retains the language supporting a Human Life Amendment to the Constitution that has been a part of it since 1980.

The Republican platform, on abortion, reads as follows:

THE SANCTITY AND DIGNITY OF HUMAN LIFE

Faithful to the "self-evident" truths enshrined in the

Declaration of Independence, we assert the sanctity of human life and affirm that the unborn child has a fundamental individual right to life which cannot be infringed.

We support a human life amendment to the Constitution and endorse legislation to make clear that the Fourteenth Amendment's protections apply to unborn children.

We oppose using public revenues to promote or perform abortion or funding organizations, which perform or advocate it and will not fund or subsidize health care, which includes abortion coverage.

We support the appointment of judges who respect traditional family values and the sanctity of innocent human life.

We oppose the non-consensual withholding or withdrawal of care or treatment, including food and water, from people with disabilities, including newborns, as well as the elderly and infirm, just as we oppose active and passive euthanasia and assisted suicide.

Republican leadership has led the effort to prohibit the barbaric practice of partial birth abortion and permitted States to extend health care coverage to children before birth.

We urge Congress to strengthen the Born Alive Infant Protection Act by exacting appropriate civil and criminal penalties to health care providers who fail to provide treatment and care to an infant who survives an abortion, including early induction delivery where the death of the infant is intended.

We call for legislation to ban sex-selective abortions, gender discrimination in its most lethal form, and to protect from abortion unborn children who are capable of feeling pain; and we applaud U.S. House Republicans for leading the effort to protect the lives of pain-capable unborn children in the District of Columbia.

We call for a revision of federal law 42 U.S.C. 289.92 to bar the use of body parts from aborted fetuses for research.

We support and applaud adult stem cell research to develop lifesaving therapies, and we oppose the killing of embryos for their stem cells.

We oppose federal funding of embryonic stem cell research.
We also salute the many states that have passed laws for informed consent, mandatory waiting periods prior to an abortion, and health protective clinic regulation.

We seek to protect young girls from exploitation through a parental consent requirement; and we affirm our moral obligation to assist, rather than penalize, women challenged by an unplanned pregnancy.

We salute those who provide them with counseling and adoption alternatives and empower them to choose life, and we take comfort in the tremendous increase in adoptions that has followed Republican legislative initiatives.

In recognition of the fact that abortion, along with other factors, is undermining the traditional nuclear family and in recognition that the American family is the basic unit of education and nurture, the Republicans adopted a strong statement on marriage as follows:

> *A serious threat to our country's constitutional order, perhaps even more dangerous than presidential malfeasance, is an activist judiciary, in which some judges usurp the powers reserved to other branches of government. A blatant example has been the court-ordered redefinition of marriage in several States.*

> *This is more than a matter of warring legal concepts and ideals. It is an assault on the foundations of our society, challenging the institution, which, for thousands of years in virtually every civilization, has been entrusted with the rearing of children and the transmission of cultural values.*

> *That is why Congressional Republicans took the lead in enacting the Defense of Marriage Act, affirming the right of States and the federal government not to recognize same-sex relationships licensed in other jurisdictions. The current Administration's open defiance of this constitutional principle, in its handling of immigration cases, in federal personnel benefits, in allowing a same-sex marriage at a military base, and in refusing to defend DOMA in the courts, makes a mockery of the President's inaugural oath.*

> *We commend the United States House of Representatives and State Attorneys General who have defended these*

laws when they have been attacked in the courts.

We reaffirm our support for a Constitutional amendment defining marriage as the union of one man and one woman. We applaud the citizens of the majority of States, which have enshrined in their constitutions the traditional concept of marriage, and we support the campaigns underway in several other States to do so.

I have no intention of sounding partisan. I am just facing the facts. Rarely has there ever been such a distinct defining difference between the two major political parties than now on moral and family value issues.

But never before have the stakes been higher as to which party controls the White House and the Congress. It makes a distinct difference. It should also be pointed out that no individual candidate or officeholder is totally defined by the political party of his or her affiliation. That's why you need to know the candidates.

Rep. Paul Ryan perhaps best summed it up in his acceptance speech:

Our different faiths come together in the same moral creed. We believe that in every life there is goodness; for every person, there is hope. Each one of us was made for a reason, bearing the image and likeness of the Lord of Life.

We have responsibilities, one to another. We do not each face the world alone. And the greatest of all responsibilities, is that of the strong to protect the weak. The truest measure of any society is how it treats those who cannot defend or care for themselves.

I also don't want to infer that being involved politically is the only way to be involved. That was my choice. It may not be yours. Do what you feel you can do best, but do something.... and make it a priority.

The goal is to change opinions, publicly, personally, privately and neighborly. If all people had the correct facts, then I believe that public opinion would change decidedly.

You can get involved and must, not just politically but in your church. Get a book like this one and have a group study. Spread the word, pick up a trumpet and start a parade. You can and must make a difference.

CHAPTER FIFTEEN

THE GOOD NEWS: WE ARE WINNING

"Commit to the Lord whatever you do, and your plans will succeed." Proverbs 16:3

I want to end this book where I began, and that is with passion for the sanctity of life; I want to end by telling you that we are winning and we will win.

Sometime in the future, either Roe will be reversed, or the abortion movement will fail for lack of support owing to a cultural shift that we already see happening.

My personal belief is that there will come a day when the twentieth and twenty-first century abortion carnage will be viewed as we now view slavery of the nineteenth century.

I believe Roe vs. Wade to be the single most insidious and socially divisive and morally destructive decisions ever in the history of American judicature. It represents the ultimate in judicial activism.

In other words, the court chose a solution and looked for law to wrap it in. It is the epitome of judicial engineering and reeks of a violation of the separation of powers clause in the constitution.

I believe that someday Roe will be overturned, just as the ruling on slavery was overturned, but between now and then there is much else that can be done... done by you and me.

As I stated before and say again, abortion is nothing less than fetal homicide and is the ultimate form of child abuse.

Former Planned Parenthood director Abby Johnson is surprised so many abortion industry employees want to follow her out the door. Johnson left her Planned Parenthood center of Bryan, Texas, in 2009 after witnessing on ultrasound the abortion of a 13-week

147

baby.

She went on to write the memoir, *Unplanned,* about her conversion to the pro-life perspective. Last June, after abortion workers had begun contacting her for help in leaving their own jobs, Johnson started an organization to support them called And Then There Were None (ATTWN). By the end of the year, ATTWN had helped 40 workers make their exits.

This is but one example of why we can and are winning the abortion culture war. The recent cover of Time Magazine could not have said it better. Forty years ago, the abortionists won with Roe v. Wade, and they have been losing ever since.

Johnson's ministry provides legal assistance, spiritual counsel, and moral and financial support for workers leaving the industry and helps them hunt for new jobs. In some cases, a worker leaving an abortion operation has a ripple effect on other employees: Six workers left a facility in Georgia, and five left one in Houston. At that rate of departure, Johnson hopes many of the nation's abortion centers will be forced to close their doors. (World 1.26.13)

Education can bring about cultural change. Think back thirty years ago when everyone smoked. Everywhere. I remember all day sessions of the legislature when by afternoon there was a cloud in the dome of the chamber.

When I was elected, my wife, whose mother was a heavy smoker and died at an early age from lung cancer, asked me to file legislation to curb smoking in specified public places.

I did, and the first year it never got out of committee, but we kept trying. Others joined the cause to fight of tobacco use. More evidence became available regarding the health dangers of smoking. Businesses began prohibiting smoking in certain areas and some banned it all together. Airlines created smoking and non-smoking sections. We significantly increased the cigarette tax.

Some of this was done by legislation such as requiring warning labels on cigarette packages, but change resulted from voluntary action based on changing the view point of the people.

What people had seen as a cigarette they now saw as a cancer stick. What had been a respite of recreation was now seen as an impediment of health, etc.

I believe that with better education, more CPC's and legislation to slow down the abortion process and provide more information and especially more abortion alternatives, we will continue to see a decline in the number of abortions in America.

With stronger, yet more user friendly, adoption laws, we will continue to see a decline in the number of abortions in America.

There is no such thing as an unwanted child. If a child is not wanted by the parents, it is wanted by someone and can be placed in a home where it can be nurtured and loved.

THERE IS NO SUCH THING AS AN UNWANTED CHILD. IF IT IS NOT WANTED BY THE PARENTS, IT IS WANTED BY SOMEONE AND CAN BE PLACED IN A HOME WHERE IT CAN BE NURTURED AND LOVED.

However, if we are to win, we need to keep hammering home the fact that IT IS A LIFE!

SHE SAYS	WE SAY
I am not married.	It is a life
A baby will keep me from getting educated.	It is a life
I already have too many children.	It is a life
The baby has physical problems.	It is a life
I am just too young to be a mother.	It is a life
I didn't ask to be pregnant. I don't want to be.	It is a life
My parents or boyfriend are forcing me to abort.	It is a life
I can't afford a baby.	It is a life
I don't know what to do with the baby after birth.	It is a life

We have to drive home the issue is life and with modern technology, we can assist in that process in so many irrefutable ways.

In the twenty-first century, politicians and women's groups started using the term "war on women" to refer to the pro-life movement to limit or restrict abortion. It is interesting that for forty years the pro-abortionists have been on the offense, but now suddenly they are on the defense. So, if it's a war, who's winning and who is losing?

Some would say that no one is winning, but I would say that we are and here is why.

Even though abortion is still legal and will be until some enlightened court reverses Roe, our side is doing an ever-better and more innovative job of making it as difficult and as slow as possible to obtain abortions. At the same time we are providing loving and caring alternatives and unbiased pre-natal education. This is in thanks, for the most part, to the CPC's.

The exciting part is what is happening in state legislatures. In 2011, some eighty abortion restrictions were passed in nineteen states. Please note that the operative words are "WERE PASSED."

The Guttmacher Institute recently released a report which found that states enacted 39 abortion restrictions in 2012. This means that 2012 was the second-most productive year in terms of the number of pro-life bills that were passed. The only year that was more productive was 2011, which saw the enactment of 80 pieces of pro-life legislation.

That means more than just filing a bill that dies on a committee calendar so a member can go home and say that they sponsored pro-life legislation. It means that a bill was filed, passed both houses and was signed into law by a governor.

We are talking about mandatory ultrasound and listening to the heartbeat, parental consent, informed consent, waiting periods, etc. Yes, these measures passed and were signed into law.

Unfortunately, a number of these laws have met their fate with temporary injunctions by the federal courts. But the point is that the people elected legislators who passed these measures, and legislators tend to follow the polls and the will of their constituents.

One measure, passed in South Dakota, would even require a mother to visit a CPC before getting an abortion.

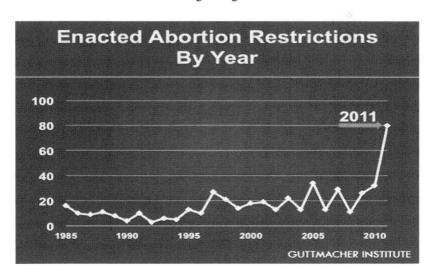

In 2013, overriding a veto from the governor, conservative lawmakers in Arkansas passed the strictest abortion ban in the country, prohibiting most abortions after twelve weeks of gestation. Nine days later, the North Dakota legislature, not to be outdone, passed its bill prohibiting abortions performed as early as six weeks.

Both bills employ a new pro-life strategy of prohibiting abortions once a baby's heart can be detected using a trans-vaginal ultrasound. Of course, both will be challenged in court. But the point is that these kinds of laws are being passed when only a few years ago, they would never have even received a hearing, let alone been passed, in most state legislatures.

In 2013 the state Senate in North Carolina passed a bill that would ban taxpayer funding for abortions, protect freedom of conscience for all healthcare professionals, and require abortion centers to meet the facility standards of ambulatory centers. Only one of the state's abortion centers currently meets those standards.

I suggest to you that when I first was elected, the public mood was two to one pro-choice, and these kinds of bills would never see the light of day. However, the public opinion numbers here significantly changed, and the attraction for legislators to take them up and pass them is a play to the home-crowd and a good one.

Look at the results of Gallup's polling on the issue of abortion over the years:

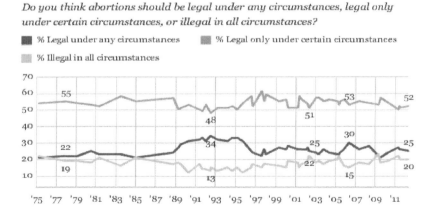

Do you think abortions should be legal under any circumstances, legal only under certain circumstances, or illegal in all circumstances?

■ % Legal under any circumstances   ■ % Legal only under certain circumstances

■ % Illegal in all circumstances

GALLUP®

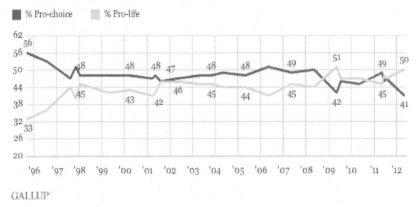

With respect to the abortion issue, would you consider yourself to be pro-choice or pro-life?

Trend from polls where pro-life/pro-choice was asked after question on legality of abortion

■ % Pro-choice   ▨ % Pro-life

GALLUP

Notice that since 1996 those who identify themselves as pro-choice have dropped from 56% to 41%, while those identifying themselves as pro-life have risen from 33% to 50%.

Here is the recent finding by the Gallup organization (May 23, 2012 "Pro-Choice" Americans at Record-Low 41% Americans now tilt "pro-life" by nine-point margin, 50% to 41% by Lydia Saad) :

> *The 41% of Americans who now identify themselves as "pro-choice" is down from 47% last July and is one percentage point below the previous record low in Gallup trends, recorded in May 2009. Fifty percent now call themselves "pro-life," one point shy of the record high, also from May 2009.*
>
> *Gallup began asking Americans to define themselves as pro-choice or pro-life on abortion in 1995, and since then, identification with the labels has shifted from a wide lead for the pro-choice position in the mid-1990's, to a generally narrower lead for "pro-choice" -- from 1998 through 2008 -- to a close division between the two positions since 2009. However, in the last period, Gallup has found the pro-life position significantly ahead on two occasions, once in May 2009 and again today. It remains*

to be seen whether the pro-life spike found this month proves temporary, as it did in 2009, or is sustained for some period.

The decline in Americans' self-identification as "pro-choice" is seen across the three U.S. political groups.

Since 2001, the majority of Republicans have consistently taken the pro-life position, but only by a gradual increasing margin over "pro-choice." That gap expanded further this year, with the percentage of Republicans identifying as pro-life increasing to 72% from 68% last May, and those identifying as pro-choice dropping to 22% from 28%.

In August of 2012, CNN, not necessarily known for taking a conservative bias, released a poll which was summed up by Life-News.com (CNN Poll: Majority of Americans Want Abortions Prohibited by Steven Ertelt Washington, DC |LifeNews.com 8/24/12) as follows:

CNN has released the results of a new poll showing a majority of Americans want all or most abortions prohibited, a clear pro-life majority. The survey asked: "Do you think abortion should be legal under any circumstances, legal under only certain circumstances, or illegal in all circumstances?" Some 62 percent want abortions illegal in all cases or legal only in certain instances while just 35% want abortions legal for any reason.

Breaking down the question further, CNN asked, "Do you think abortion should be legal in most circumstances or only a few circumstances?" Here, 52 percent took a pro-life view saying abortion should be illegal in all (15%) or most circumstances (37%) while just 44 percent took a pro-abortion view saying abortions should be legal in all (35%) or most (9%) circumstances.

Looking more closely at when abortions should be

legal, CNN asked about if they should be allowed when the woman's life is endangered. Americans agreed by an 88-9 percentage point margin. In cases of rape and incest, Americans supported legal abortions on an 83-14 percentage point margin. And when the woman's health is supposedly in danger from the pregnancy, Americans were alright with abortion on an 83-12 percentage point margin. The polls make it clear Americans only support abortion in the rarest instances and clearly oppose abortions in the 99 percent of cases when abortion is chosen for convenience, social or birth control reasons.

Not only are the public opinion numbers swinging in the pro-life direction, but the number of procedures is down as well. In Florida, laws passed in 2010 caused a significant decrease in the number of abortions in the state, as reported by Sunshine State News. (June 2, 2012).

As Year-Old Laws Take Hold, Abortions Tumble in Florida

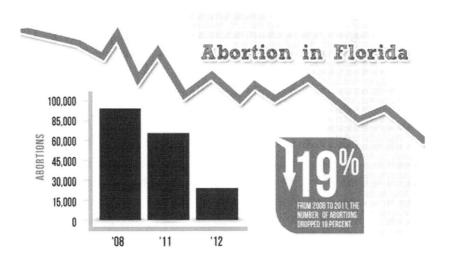

All figures were provided by the state Agency for Health Care

Administration.

The number of Florida abortion clinics has also dwindled. There reportedly are now some 70 abortion providers in the state -- nearly 30 percent fewer than in 2005.

State legislators take some of the credit for the decrease, citing tougher regulations on abortion clinics.

Requiring the basics of emergency medical care and tightening requirements on places that are performing surgical procedures is a good and necessary step. Prior to the legislation, some of the basics weren't even done. If these eliminated clinics are forced out of business because of substandard practice, that's a good thing.

In 2011 the Legislature passed and Gov. Rick Scott signed a bill requiring ultrasounds before women can obtain abortions.

Since Jan. 1, 2011, Florida laws also stipulate:

- The parent of a minor must be notified before an abortion is provided.
- Public funding is available for abortion only in cases of life endangerment, rape or incest.
- Health plans that will be offered in the state's health exchange that will be established under the federal health care reform law can only cover abortion in cases of rape or incest when the woman's life is endangered, unless an optional rider is purchased at an additional cost.

The bottom line is that when the laws are tougher, abortion numbers are going to decrease as they have in Florida, and that has been repeated in state after state. This progress was unthinkable not that many years ago.

Organizations like the Florida Ethics and Religious Liberty Commission, along with other pro-life and pro-family organizations, are coming together and gathering support which is backed up by many voters and cannot be ignored by legislators.

Public opinion is being driven by events such as the conviction of Dr. Kermit Gosnell. He was found guilty on three counts of killing babies born alive during abortions and one count of involuntary manslaughter in the death of a woman who died from complications as a result of an abortion. He was also found guilty of several hundred lesser crimes, such as fraud and conspiracy. He waived appeal in exchange for escaping the death penalty.

The verdict brings a level of justice for those who died in what local prosecutors called the Philadelphia "house of horrors." The public was outraged in the fact that state authorities failed to inspect the facility for almost twenty years, allowing the victimization of women through unsanitary conditions and the murder of babies born alive in the name of "choice."

Unfortunately, the media did not give the story the coverage it deserved, but it did expose what happens behind closed doors in the abortion industry. After the trial two U.S. House committees launched investigations into how diligently states are enforcing pro-life laws and regulating abortion sellers. State attorneys general and health department officials have been asked to provide detailed information as to how they are tracking and monitoring this industry.

Even many who call themselves pro-choice were shocked at the facts. It is interesting that a majority of the members of the Gosnell jury said they were pro-choice.

Not surprisingly, the pro-abortion crowd was quick to blame Gosnell's brutal offenses on, of all things, the restrictions on the abortion facilities.

How typical: Abortion activists will do anything to change the conversation. They gloss over the fact that abortion ends a human life.

It has been a long battle, and it won't be over soon, but we are moving in the right direction. A war is not won with a single battle, and we have to be satisfied to win it piece by piece, law by law and court by court.

Notwithstanding the roadblocks put up by the courts, there have been victories.

For example, the abortion industry now realizes that state legislatures are not as friendly, so they have turned to local government for help. They have sought to require CPC's to post various disclaimers that would tend to discourage women from using their services.

In 2010, in Montgomery County Maryland, the County Council approved a regulation requiring the posting of disclaimers like "The center does not have a licensed medical professional on staff," and "The Montgomery County Health Officer encourages women who are or may be pregnant to consult with a licensed health care provider." The penalty for failing to post the disclaimers was $750 per day.

The law was struck down by the federal court, saying: "The government, even with the purest of motives, may not substitute its judgment as to how to best speak for that of speakers and listeners."

As a matter of fact, the CPC involved in the Maryland case (Centro Tepeyac) made contact with more than 3,000 women and assisted fifty-nine abortion-minded women who changed their mind and chose life. Not only did that save those babies' lives, but it took fifty-nine abortions away from the abortion industry. That may not sound like many, but there are an estimated three thousand plus CPC's nationally, and that is many lives saved. (A Quiet Victory for Life – and The First Amendment, by Gary Bauer, Human Events, July 9,2012)

Here is the real point: the mere existence of these pregnancy center regulations is an acknowledgement by the abortion industry that these centers are successful in their mission and that they are one of the primary reasons abortion figures have been on the decline.

The abortion industry appears to have harmed itself with sex-selection abortion. The pro-life investigative group Live Action (liveaction.org) released devastating evidence that the nation's largest abortion provider systemically engages in the grisly practice of sex-selection abortion, a charge to which it now admits.

Let's put aside for a moment the scandalous disclosure that while the nation's largest abortion provider receives over 350 million per annum in your taxpayer dollars, it nonetheless spends millions engaging in partisan politicking for pro-abortion laws and other government support.

Troubling as that may be, utterly horrific is the revelation that this organization, which presumes to defend "women's rights," has been caught red-handed torturing little girls to death in their mother's womb, simply because the mother wanted a boy.

So disturbing are the facts that in the summer of 2012, the U.S. House of Representatives voted on the Prenatal Non-Discrimination Act (PRENDA), H.R. 354, introduced in Congress. Unbelievably, because the bill required a two-thirds majority for passage, pro-abortion legislators were able to narrowly defeat the measure by a vote of 246-168. The legislation, which would have outlawed sex-selection abortions altogether, was also opposed by the President.

This entire saga has placed the irreconcilable incongruities central to our nation's ongoing policy of legalized abortion-on-demand in the national spotlight.

Matt Barber, in his column, Equal Rights for Unborn Feminists (http://www.wnd.com/2012/06/equal-rights-for-unborn-feminists/) provides the following example:

> Consider, for instance, that under current federal and state law, if an off-duty abortionist, if any man, for that matter, physically assaults a woman and her unborn daughter dies, that man has committed murder. Yet, if mom walks into Planned Parenthood and authorizes that same man to rip her baby girl limb-from-limb, it's her

"choice." First case: murder. Second case: "choice." Both cases: dead baby girl.

Furthermore, consider that, as established by a 2006 Zogby International poll of over 30,000 Americans in 48 states, 86 percent support a law banning sex-selection abortion. Doesn't it stand to reason, then, that since the vast majority recognizes the objectively reprehensible nature of sex-selection abortion, they, too, might recognize that it's equally reprehensible for mom to have baby killed for no reason at all? This is what current law allows, without restriction, through the ninth month.

Indeed, incongruities abound. Still, it is the indefensible nature of empty "pro-choice" rhetoric that, I believe, will ultimately end legalized abortion in America.

Truth, even when buried for decades, eventually has a way of rising to the surface.

It's inevitable. Roe v. Wade will, in time, be tossed, alongside the slavery-justifying Dred Scott decision. That is exactly where both shameful scars on Lady Liberty belong…in the trash heap of historical inhumanity.

Just as those who excused slavery are reviled by history, so, too, will be those who called themselves "pro-choice."

It is inevitable and only a matter of time when this horrible practice of abortion on demand will be history. The industry has pushed the envelope too far. Even those who consider themselves pro-choice for basic early abortions are incensed with procedures like the brutal partial birth abortion, gender selection and the like.

Partial birth abortion has gone even further than I believe the Roe court would have envisioned. Technically known as a D & X abortion, it is used in late second and third trimesters (24-36 weeks). Forceps are introduced into the uterus to grasp the baby's legs.

The baby is delivered breech while the head remains inside the birth canal (technically unborn). Using blunt-tipped surgical scissors, the base of the skull is pierced and a suction catheter is inserted to extract the brain. This causes the skull to collapse and the dead baby is then fully delivered.

Planned Parenthood and the industry in general have over-played their hand. I personally believe that ultimately to be on the wrong side of Planned Parenthood will be on the right side of history.

As people are educated through crisis pregnancy centers and the like, the numbers are changing. Abortions are in decline. Polls show the pro-life numbers to be gaining and pro-choice numbers are retreating. Meanwhile, lawmakers who closely follow the polls as an effective means of getting re-elected are leaning our way more and more.

We simply cannot let up and must keep the pressure on. We must elect pro-life lawmakers and defeat those who oppose our position. We must more than ever support, fund, and build up the crisis pregnancy centers.

Churches must become more involved, and they don't have to get in the political endorsement process to do so. They can edu-cate members on the issues and on the horrors of abortion and let everyone know where candidates stand on the issue. This needs to become a litmus test issue for every candidate in every election.

A candidate not firmly pro-life and not committed to voting that way is not worthy of my vote or yours, and they need to know it.

We need to educate. We need to participate. But lastly, we need to pray, strongly and daily. Commit it to God. Yes, it is a legal and a culture war, but ultimately it is God's war to protect the lives he so uniquely created. It is perhaps best summed up in Brad Bright's book, God is the Issue (Bright Media Foundation, p 141):

I am saying the battles of our moral sanity are ultimately doomed to failure if we do not engage the culture in a simultaneous conversation about who God really is and why it matters. It is time to unapologetically hijack every cultural symptom as a platform for making God the issue in the public square just as Jesus, Peter and Paul did. No matter the question, it is time to reframe the pivotal issue as God.

God is the issue and God grieves whenever one of his own is taken in the name of choice. Abortion has to stop. Abortion will stop, if everyone who reads these words steps up to the plate and joins the team of life; for at the end of the day the issue is life.

May we not just curse the darkness of abortion, but may we light candles of life and provide the oxygen to make them burn.

Never, never forget that the issue is life.

SENATOR JOHN GRANT

Senator John Grant is an attorney, writer, teacher, speaker and a former state senator. He has practiced law for more than forty years, served on the faculty of two universities, and served as an instructor for the United States Peace Corps. He holds three earned and two honorary degrees.

In his public service, President Ronald Reagan appointed him to the Graduate Fellow Board in the United States Department of Education. President Nixon also appointed him to serve on the Advisory Council of the Small Business Administration. He has been twice appointed to the Florida Commission on Ethics, where he served as Vice Chairman.

Governor Jeb Bush appointed him to serve as Executive Director of the Office of Statewide Public Guardianship, where he oversaw the statewide program for providing guardianship services for Florida's indigent citizens. For his work on behalf of the elderly and disabled, he was named to the National Senior Citizen Hall of Fame and has been recognized as one of the top Legislators in America for mental health issues. He was named to Who's Who in America.

During his twenty-one years as a member of the Florida Legislature, he was nationally recognized for his relentless fight to protect the right to life for the unborn. He authored and passed the first legislation in America defining marriage as a union between a man and a woman.

Now retired from elective office, he has traded the Senate chamber for the podium to train, educate and motivate people to save lives of the unborn.

His weekly writings are read electronically by thousands around the world.

Active in his church, he has been listed in Who's Who in

American Religion. In his local church, Idlewild Baptist, he is an ordained deacon, having served as Chairman, served on multiple committees and served as a Bible Fellowship teacher.

Long active in Bible publishing and distribution, he has been on the board of American Bible Society for more than thirty years and has served as Chairman of the Committee on Governance and of the Strategic Directions Committee.

For four years, he was a member of and chaired the America's Board of the United Bible Societies and frequently spoke and taught in countries throughout Central and South America helping Bible Societies in their work and organization.

In his spare time, he enjoys hunting white tail deer in South Carolina, traveling, and most of all, spending time with his wife, Beverley, and their three children and nine grandchildren.

7.12.13